Reform or Revolt

A Push to End Discrimination in our Banks and Financial Institutions Based on Economic Class, Race, Sex and for Being Differently Abled

By Benjamin Davis, MBA
bendavis9@hotmail.com

For Grace and Warren and a million possibilities.

Contents

Prologue
1. Customer Rights
2. Income Inequality
3. Risk-based Pricing
4. Credit Scores
5. DTI
6. LTV
7. PMI
8. Alternative Financing – Payday and Title Loans
9. Bank Fees
10. Costs
11. Reform
12. Revolt!
13. Just the Beginning

About the Author
Bibliography

Prologue

My latest role in finance was one of a vice president with one of the largest banks in the world. As a bank Sr. Business Control Specialist, my manager encouraged me to address the why, who, what, where, how and when questions when identifying issues and designing solutions for bank services and processes. I will take that good man's advice to heart as I begin this book.

Why did I write this book?

There is a dream still not fully realized. As long as income inequality remains the norm for business and as long as financial institutions do not account for wage disparity in their policies and decisions, then it will remain only a dream. One forever out of reach.

This book is intended to first identify the financial discrimination that is part of our everyday financial culture in banking and payday and title loan stores. That is covered in chapters 1 – 10. Chapter 11 focuses on how financial institutions can resolve the issue. Chapter 12 covers how the public can encourage financial institutions to resolve the issue.

Who did I write this book for?

This book was written with financial institutions and their customers as the intended audience.

I am recommending changes to current policies and routines that I believe will increase the revenue of financial institutions and decrease their risk of lawsuits and fines due to discriminatory practices.

I am making these recommendations on behalf of those who are being discriminated against because of current financial policies. That includes:

> Low and middle tier wage earners of any race or sex
> All differently abled individuals

What was I hoping to gain by writing this book?

To continue a public conversation on financial discrimination that will hopefully move us closer to ending this destructive practice. Our citizens, financial institutions and the economy of our entire country is being held back because of income inequality and financial institutions that enhance its damaging effects. We could achieve more, increase profits, and improve the overall quality of life for millions if we discriminated less.

An end to financial discrimination will allow people a greater chance to realize their dreams and become their full potential. It should also increase the profitability of financial institutions and businesses. We grow best when we grow together.

Where can the ideas in this book be applied?

In every financial institution. Every day financial discrimination is occurring in every financial institution in our country. It is so deeply imbedded in current policies and accepted norms that it is not currently recognized for what it truly is. This book attempts to unmask those practices as discriminatory.

How can the ideas in this book be applied?

Financial institutions will find a list of recommendations in chapter 11. This includes details on how to implement. I know changing policies and procedures takes time, requires difficult choices and sacrifices. However, it must start somewhere. It must start with someone; a true leader that knows there are greater returns for those that act first. Those that act last are forgotten first.

The public will find a list of ideas in chapter 12 that they can take action on to make their voices heard. It is important that financial institutions know that they have your support in making changes to end financial discrimination. In this image-centric time in which we find ourselves, business policy follows public demand.

When can the ideas in this book be applied?

Immediately. Our citizens and economy have been suppressed by financial discrimination for too long. It is time to unlock the full potential of American ingenuity, imagination and innovation. It is time for *Reform or Revolt*.

A special note to financial institutions before we begin. The ideas in this book are my own. They are the issues I have identified and solutions I am recommending to solve for discrimination in our banks and financial industry. However, there are a lot of brilliant people in the financial industry and innovation has become our trademark. If you can design a better solution that resolves financial discrimination and levels the playing field for everyone regardless of economic class, race, sex or for being differently abled, then you have my full support. But as long as wage disparities exist and financial decisions are judged equally for a group of citizens that are not paid equally or hired equally or promoted equally, then discrimination will remain a part of our financial institutions and it is the responsibility of all citizens to push for change.

Chapter 1

Customer Rights

"…We hold these truths to be self-evident, that all (wo)men are created equal, that they are endowed by their Creator with certain unalienable Rights, that among these are Life, Liberty and the pursuit of Happiness.."

– Declaration of Independence for the United States of America

In order to protect "all (wo)men" and promote the "unalienable Rights" defined in the Declaration of Independence, those of Life and Liberty and the pursuit of Happiness, I believe financial institutions have a constitutional responsibility to:

1. Provide equal access to all financial services without exclusion based on a person's economic class, race, sex or if they are differently abled.
2. Provide equal terms for all loans and deposit products without variance based on a person's economic class, race, sex or if they are differently abled.

> ➢ I define financial discrimination as when either of these two responsibilities are not met.

A majority of the U.S. population is experiencing discrimination in banks and financial institutions on a daily basis. Many do not even realize that they are. That discrimination includes classism, racism, sexism and ableism. Much of it is legal. It is widely accepted. It is institutionalized in every bank and credit union and impacts payday and title loan customers. And it is killing us.

Let's use a visualization exercise to understand current financial practices. Imagine two groups of people eating the exact same meal at the same exact restaurant. The wealthy white men pay $15 for their respective meal. The poor white men, the black men, the women and the differently abled are charged $22.50 for the same meal.

If this restaurant scenario were true it would be outrageous! People would be protesting outside of the eatery with signs about equality and human rights. Politicians would sprint to the nearest news camera to condemn the unfair practice (and try to win a few votes for the next election). Candlelight vigils would be held with large, ethnically diverse groups of people locking arms and singing for change.

Thankfully I do not know of a single restaurant that is charging different prices for their food based on economic class, race, sex or for being differently abled. If someone identifies one let me know and I will join in the march against them.

However, banks and credit unions in our country are charging different prices for their services based on economic class, race, sex or for a person being differently abled. It is happening each day in every financial location. So where is the outrage?

Financial institutions are charging higher loan rates and making fee decisions based on credit decisions and account usage influenced by data that is biased against economic class, race, sex and physical ability. The difference in prices could add up to one person paying over $100,000 more over their lifetime for the same house and cars that their neighbor purchased. The difference in price being based on the color of the applicant's skin, their gender or because they are differently abled. That is money that could have been spent on college education for their children or for starting a business. Whereas the person might have struggled to keep food on the table and to keep the lights on, an extra $100,000 could have lessened their burden and could have changed the trajectory of their life and that of their descendants for generations.

The weapons for this type of financial discrimination are risk-based pricing of loans, loan-to-value calculations, debt-to-income calculations and required insurance policies for only some individuals. Bank fees are also subject to bias and can be either waived or charged based on discriminatory factors. All of this will be examined throughout this book as well as examples of how different groups of people are negatively impacted by the various weapons of financial discrimination. It will get technical at times but I will attempt to make it both understandable and relatable.

This book continues a war that has been fought, for too many generations, over integration versus separate but equal. Equal being a full integration of every economic class, race, gender and people who are differently abled into the fabric of society. An integration of humanity; to recognize the God-given value of an individual and to celebrate our differences rather than using them to vilify and degrade and disenfranchise.

I stand in awe of the bravery and restraint of those that have fought for integration. There is no greater test of strength than to meet hatred with love, ignorance with patience. And the men and women who fought on the front lines of integration and inclusion (and those that still do) are the heroes we must remember and seek to emulate.

The separate but equal philosophy is blatant discrimination. There is no other reason to keep one group of God's children away from another group of God's children. Other excuses have been derived but they are all thin veils over the doctrine of hate. And whereas I have a lot to say on this subject, other, more talented writers and activists can express it better. But I will say that in many respects separate but equal was replaced by an unspoken philosophy of same but unequal.

Remember the restaurant in our example before, the one that was charging higher prices for their food based on a person's economic class, race, sex or physical ability? The restaurant was not practicing the separate but equal ideology because they were "willing" to serve anyone in their restaurant. However, they were obviously still not treating people fairly. Now what if they changed tactics? What if the public outcry was so loud that they were forced to take action? Could that restaurant still cater to predominantly rich white men in a way that would not be obvious and would still be compliant with federal law? Sadly, the answer is yes.

Early in my banking career I was taught that banks price for the type of business they want. If the bank receives low risk, large lending requests (i.e. a secured business loan with a well-qualified customer) they may put out a promotional price on certificates of deposits or other savings accounts to raise the sum needed for the loans. If the bank prefers to not make used auto loans then they will carry higher interest rates on used car loans so as to dissuade applicants from applying for those types of loans. Everything is regulated by price.

In our restaurant example, the restaurant could also price to exclude customers they do not want to serve. Knowing that minorities and women and the differently abled tend to make less money than white men, the restaurant could raise the price on their $15 meal to $75. This would exclude poor white people from eating at their restaurant as well. It would be a lawful and accepted practice for restaurants to raise their prices in this way. But since it prices out most people who are counting pennies, it can be considered same but unequal. Same because anyone is allowed to eat there. Unequal because prices were raised to purposely exclude a select population.

Banks and credit unions do the same thing. They price to exclude the customers they do not want. And as will be detailed later in this book, the reasons for exclusion pricing are based on economic class, race, sex, and physical ability.

Same but unequal ideology is an evil practice that must end. It profits the few at the expense of the many. It prevents people from reaching their full potential by limiting their opportunities.

> ➢ Need an affordable car to get back and forth to work?
>
> The interest rate on your car is too high because of the color of your skin and now you have to skip meals to make the payments.
>
> ➢ Need to move into a house in a safe neighborhood to raise your children?
>
> You were not born rich and therefore your loan-to-value is too high and you are forced to

pay hundreds more every month on insurance to protect the bank in case you default.

- Want to go to college and need a private loan to cover costs?

  You cannot get the loan because you are a woman and face income inequality. You will not be attending college nor getting any job that requires a college degree.

- Need to start a business because you cannot find a job?

  Not happening because you were born differently abled.

There are laws in place to protect all of us from direct discrimination – denying your loan or raising interest rate prices based solely because of the color of your skin, or your economic class, or your gender or physical ability. Banks and credit unions hide behind those laws and their own policies which state the same. However, they make lending and pricing decisions based on data that is influenced by economic class, race, sex, and physical ability. Therefore, it is indirect discrimination and is easily proven in the chapters ahead.

Indirect discrimination is like money laundering. It allows you to take an illegal activity and legitimize it through a layer of process that is both legal and acceptable. The only difference is that our legal system considers money laundering illegal, whereas indirect discrimination is not.

For banks and other financial institutions, indirect discrimination is very profitable. And because banks and credit unions make billions of dollars in profits every year through pricing related to indirect discrimination, I doubt they will change policy willingly. Chances are, it will take a concerted effort of ordinary citizens demanding change, and laws to support those changes, before banks and credit unions take action.

The benefit to consumers for financial institutions to change their discriminatory practices is obvious. Less money spent on loans means more money can be spent on meeting basic and educational needs. Consumers can spend more on revitalizing their communities, starting businesses, living their dreams.

There is a large incentive for banks and credit unions to end discrimination as well. When consumers have billions more, it means larger savings balances for the banks. And when more consumers are starting businesses and buying houses and cars, the bank will sell more loans and make more of a profit.

Ending financial discrimination is a win-win scenario.

A disclaimer before we move on. When I speak of the inequality in banking and involving other financial institutions, I am speaking of overall company policies and processes and the changes that need to take place. I am not criticizing the thousands of employees who are working in good faith. Many of them do not see the correlation between their daily duties and the financial discrimination that influences their work.

Many of my former teammates were hard working and honest people. A few of them had less than ideal personalities, but most were generous and kind. Many donated of their time to better their communities and worked hard to provide fair lending and banking services to their friends and family and neighbors. Many of the bankers I worked with were also part of a group of people discriminated against because of economic class, race, sex or physical ability. I still proudly consider many of my former teammates as friends. And I hope this book helps them understand how they can make a positive difference in their current role.

Financial institutions also do good for their community. They donate money to the communities where they operate and their employees volunteer of their time. Financial institutions are necessary for the flow of money between consumers and businesses and to provide financing for the goals and dreams of our lives. I will not argue against the existence of banks or credit unions nor deny that many good people work there. Rather, certain processes must change in order for banks and all financial institutions to serve everyone in their communities.

I have said it before and will restate it several times throughout this book, we grow best when we grow together.

A quick note on the terminology about to be used. Throughout this book I am referring to classifications of "race" and referring to skin color such as "black" or "white". This is a practice I am uncomfortable with. However, throughout this book I am referencing data from U.S. Census reports. Within those reports we are classified as "black" and "white". In an effort to not confuse the lessons learned from the data presented I have kept the same terminology. If you personally prefer to identify under another term, I apologize. I do not intend to offend.

Also, please keep in mind what I am referring to as "differently abled". This covers a broad range of individuals. Broadly speaking, it refers to anyone whose life is impacted by what some would call a disability. This could be a person born with autism, an army vet suffering from an amputation, a deaf person, etc. I believe that everyone has strengths and everyone has a purpose. That is why I refer to this group as simply having a different ability than some. Unfortunately, they too face discrimination, referred to as ableism, in their everyday lives.

Chapter 2

Income Inequality

Broadly speaking, when I use the term "income inequality", I am referring to the differences in average pay between different races, genders and whether or not a person is differently abled. Multiple reports have proven the existence of these wage gaps, including U.S. Government reports as well as reports by independent agencies. However, the percentages of income inequality vary somewhat between reports.

For this book, I am using U.S. government census data on household income, a nonpartisan report (Senega, Fontenot, & Kollar, 2017). For income data related to those with a disability, I am using another nonpartisan report supplied by AIR (American Institutes for Research, 2014). At the time of writing this book, these reports represent the most recent data points. These reports show:

- Black workers earn only 64% of what white workers earn
- Female workers earn only 80% of what male workers earn
- Workers who are differently abled only earn 63% of what non-differently abled workers earn
- White workers only earn 76% of what Asian workers earn
- Hispanic workers only earn 77% of what white workers earn

A lot has been written already on the issue of income inequality. Possible factors that have been identified to explain wage gaps have included:

- Differences in a worker's educational level
- Differences in a worker's geographical location

- Racism, sexism and ableism in hiring
- Racism, sexism and ableism in promoting

Later in this book we will explore how discrimination within our banks and financial institutions can lead to differences in a worker's educational level and geographical location as detailed above. This means that income inequality is impacted by discrimination in our financial institutions, just as financial institutions are impacted by income inequality. It is a cycle of discrimination that fuels itself and leaves a large percentage of the U.S. population forever reaching, never grasping. Always falling short of financial independence and being prevented from fully realizing their American dream just because of the color of their skin, their gender or because they are differently abled.

Throughout this book we will discuss banking and financial institution practices that are impacted by, and contribute to, discriminatory behavior. We will use 5 people to show the impact of those practices on different citizens based on their economic class, race, sex or their being differently abled. For that I need to introduce you to the 5 customer groups. So that we can have fair comparisons, we are making them the same age - 25, all are single, and all of them have the same career - marketing.

The differences we will explore are based on:

- Parental economic class
- Race
- Sex
- If differently abled

  1. William Cook is a white male. His parents are very wealthy.

2. Daniel Smith is also a white male. His parents are considered the working poor.

3. Bryan Johnson is a black male. His parents have middle class jobs and income.

4. Laura Winger is female. Her mom has a middle-class job and income. Father is deceased.

5. Christian Robinson was born with autism. His parents have middle class jobs and income but little money saved due to the extra expenses of raising a child who is differently abled.

These 5 groups represent some of those impacted by discrimination in our financial institutions but in no way is the list exhaustive or as complex as I would like. Missing from these examples are Hispanic Americans, Asian Americans, Native Americans, those that prefer to be defined by their sexual preference, those that prefer to be identified by their religion, etc.

The complexity missing in these examples is when an individual is classified under more than one group. For example, when a person is a black female who is Muslim. Or maybe an individual is a male Asian American who is differently abled. None of us fit neatly in any one category. That is what it means to be an individual. But I have chosen these 5 basic examples to start the discussion on financial discrimination based on the data that is available and to prevent overwhelming the reader with following 100 + examples in every chapter.

Let me set the record straight. I believe any discrimination is evil and must be ended. And the recommendations I make throughout this book are aimed at ending financial discrimination for all impacted groups, not just those represented by my 5 customer examples.

Now to continue our examination of the 5 customer examples we defined earlier. We know from the reports detailed earlier, that there are differences in income between peoples categorized based on their race, gender, and for being differently abled.

Using these statistics as what occurs in the majority of instances, we would expect William and Daniel to make the same initial income. We can expect Bryan to earn only 64% of what William and Daniel make. Laura would earn 80% of what William and Daniel make. And Christian would only make 63% of what William and Daniel would make. I understand that these are averages. Not every person to person comparison will validate these exact percentages. I am sure examples can be found where the wage gap is not as significant. But I am also sure examples can be found where the wage gap is even wider. We will be working off of this data as representative of the overall wage gap of which research has proven, even if the percentages change somewhat from report to report.

In the examples we laid out, let's assume William and Daniel start out with an annual salary of $40,000. Therefore our 5 examples would currently look like:

1. William is a white male that comes from a wealthy family and makes $40,000/annually.

2. Daniel is a white male that comes from a poor family and makes $40,000/annually.

3. Bryan is a black male that makes $25,600/annually.

4. Laura is female and makes $32,000/annually.

5. Christian has autism and makes $25,200/annually.

The wage gap that exists between different ethnic groups and between men and women is real, verifiable and destructive. This one imbalance in our society impacts everything else. There cannot be complete reform of any other societal issue until this travesty is recognized and resolved.

Wage gaps reflect discriminatory practices in education, housing, the financial industry, etc. In short, they reflect the lack of equal opportunities given to people based on economic class, race, sex or for being differently abled. For the purposes of this book, we are focusing on the financial industry as that is my area of expertise.

So, you ask why income inequality should matter to everyone in our country and not just to those making less money? You mean other than because it is morally reprehensible and indefensible? Because the ramifications of wage gaps can be felt in our financial institutions, our schools, our hospitals, our churches, our prisons, our government, our neighborhoods. In my opinion, which some research data supports, income inequality leads to an increase in crime. It results in an increase in drug use. It results in an increase in suicide rates when combined with mental illness. It limits the potential of so many would be Einstein's and Steve Jobs.

Imagine a person chokes to death and 3 coroners are called in to examine the body to verify the cause of death. The first coroner comes in and starts by examining the heart and states the problem is that the heart stopped beating. The second coroner comes in and examines the brain and states the problem is that the brain stopped functioning. The third coroner comes in and states the problem is that the lungs stopped working. All three would be right, those were all big problems. However, all three would have missed the bigger picture. The patient's heart and brain and lungs stopped as a result of the food lodged in the windpipe. They were not the cause of death. They were the evidence of death.

Just as in the example above, we look to other parts in our society and say the education system is broken, we need health care and prison reform, we are too divided, etc. But we are missing the bigger picture. Financial independence is the lifeblood of any society. When any people are treated unfairly and are suppressed from bettering their own lives through hard work and ingenuity, it is a poison that seeps into every aspect of society. So, of course we are divided as a nation. Income inequality puts us in competition over factors we cannot control.

There is no simple solution to fixing income inequality. It must be resolved in our health care system, schools, legal system and in every business in America. Those areas are outside of the scope of this book but may be the focus of my second book. For now, I want to focus on financial institutions because that is the gateway through which all finances pass and where I have my expertise.

Financial institutions must do more to "level the playing field". They need to recognize that income inequality is real and make policy decisions that will negate the impact of income inequality as much as possible. Instead, banking and financial institution policies enhance the damaging impact of income inequality. We will explore those practices in the chapters ahead.

Chapter 3

Risk-Based Pricing

Risk-based pricing is the practice of charging different interest rate prices to different borrowers based on the perceived risk of that borrower defaulting on their loan. It consists of looking into an applicant's past and present for clues on their possible future. It is a financial institution's version of gazing into a crystal ball to see what might be.

Those borrowers that are perceived to be of less risk to default are given the lowest interest rates. Everyone else is charged a higher interest rate.

You can qualify to pay the lowest interest rate if:

- You have made all past loan and utility and medical payments on time (reflected in your overall credit score that will be covered in a future chapter)

- You have not needed an excessive amount of loans or credit cards (reflected in your overall credit score)

- You have established a positive credit history (this will be covered in a future chapter)

- You have money set aside in a savings account

- You have not recently changed jobs or addresses

- You make enough money that you can easily pay back the loan (covered in the chapter DTI)

- You have enough money that you can make a cash down payment on your purchase for a secured loan (covered in the chapter LTV)

- The house or car that you are purchasing is considered to be of a value greater than the loan amount you request (covered in the chapter LTV)

For all those that meet the above criteria they will most likely receive a bank or credit union's lowest loan interest rate. All others will be charged higher interest rates. That translates into higher monthly payments for those that are considered of greater risk to default and not pay back their full loan. Even if those individuals have always paid off their debts in the past, the other criteria will still force them to pay higher interest rates.

What does all of the criteria above have in common? It offers the lowest monthly payments to those that least need a loan; those that can most afford a new loan. It punishes those that are struggling financially by straddling them with higher monthly loan payments.

Who is the population that would have the lowest need for loans? Those that make the most income; those who come from wealthier families and typically receive additional financial help. In our examples from the previous chapter, if William was just starting out and was going to be late on a utility payment, then his parents could make the payment for him. That protects his credit score.

What if Daniel was going to be late on his utility payment? His parents did not have enough money to make the payment for him. Therefore, Daniel's credit takes a hit, not to mention he might lose his electricity. Good luck getting ready for work in the dark. Good luck washing your clothes or shaving or charging your cell phone. God help you if you have kids at the time and have to care for them during that nightmare.

Let's look at it from a different angle. What is the population that needs loans the most? Those that make the least income. In other words, those that are most impacted by income inequality.

In the previous chapter we discussed income inequality based on economic class, race, sex and physical ability. So, if Laura works at the same company William does but makes less just because she is a woman (perhaps based on gender discrimination in the way a company promotes from within), then she could end up being considered more at risk of default because of her debt- to-income ratio calculation (this will be covered in more detail in the chapter for DTI). That risk consideration could cause Laura to pay a higher monthly payment. So, whereas William could owe $400 a month to buy a used car, Laura could have to pay $425 a month to buy the same car. That adds up to Laura paying an extra $1,800 over the next 6 years for the same vehicle for reasons related to her being a woman.

Laura's example was a modest one. Let's look at a possible subprime lending example.

Say Daniel wants to buy the same used car as Laura and William. Again, his parents are very poor and cannot help him. Daniel has been behind on a few utility payments but always paid them, eventually. He also fell behind a couple of times on his rent. He has decent income so debt-to-income will not be an issue (loan-to-value ratios may be a problem but we will discuss that later). However, he has little credit and the late payments on his utilities and rent flag him as high risk. Daniel is still approved for the loan but with little positive credit history he is approved under subprime.

Subprime are loans made to what are considered the riskiest of borrowers. They also have the highest interest rates that are offered at banks and credit unions. In fact, because of the perceived risk, the financial institutions that make subprime loans offer them through a different division of the bank. This population is not allowed to mingle with the general population.

Daniel could be approved for his car loan under a subprime rate of say 25% interest. So, whereas William is paying $400 per month for the same car and Laura is paying $425, Daniel could end up paying $675 per month for the same car. Over the span of the 6-year loan, Daniel could end up paying $19,800 more than William for the same car.

Let that sink in for a minute. A car that costs $25,000 on the lot would end up costing William $29,000 and would cost Daniel $44,800. Does that seem fair? Same car, same original cost, driven to the same job...but because William's parents could financially help him out and Daniel's could not, then Daniel is stuck paying $675 per month for the same car.

At least Daniel makes the same income as William. If he is forced to pay $675 per month for a car loan, he will still have ~$2,650 a month to pay taxes and rent and utilities and food bills and insurance, etc. He might be able to manage. What if Christian had been approved for the same car under the same subprime rate? His parents were also not wealthy and Christian's autism makes it hard for him to remember to make all of his payments exactly on the due date.

Christian's car payment would be the same as Daniel's, $675 per month. But due to the wage gap for people who are differently abled, Christian makes less than Daniel. That means after he pays the $675 monthly car loan payment, he will only have $1,425 left per month to pay taxes and rent and utilities and food bills and insurance, etc. That is not enough money to live off of and his parents cannot afford to help him make the payments. So, at some point Christian must make a decision, to make the car payment or to eat. I would hope that all of us in that position would choose food, especially if we also had children at home with hungry stomachs. The car payment would have to wait. Christian's credit gets worse.

    Imagine the example above in a different way. Think of a major league baseball game. A huge player steps up to home plate. He picks up his bat. He is the home run king in the middle of a season where he has already broken the all-time home run record (a record I still consider to belong to the greatest baseball player of all time - Hank Aaron). Then suddenly the outfield wall pops up and zooms across the grass and settles back down just behind the bases. Now imagine a little skinny kid comes up to bat next. He has never hit a home run in his life. The outfield wall pops up and goes back to its original position at the back of the outfield. Does the home run king have an unfair advantage? Is the skinny kid setup to fail? Would baseball fans riot in the stadium at such disparate treatment?

That is the basis for risk-based pricing. The goal is put further out of reach for those that are less likely to win. The financial institution does not just foresee who might fail to make their loan payments, they practically guarantee it by overcharging those that are the most vulnerable.

As we see in the examples above, risk-based pricing makes it so financial institutions make loans more unaffordable for those most at risk. It is like they are making a self-fulfilling prophecy. "Christian is high risk for defaulting on his loan. So, let's charge him extra to ensure he fails". Why would banks do this? Two reasons; for greater profit and because they legally can.

What happens if someone defaults on their loan? The financial institution repossesses the asset (a car in our example above). Then the financial institution will sell the asset (perhaps at auction or through their own efforts such as through a bank website listing). They are not concerned with getting top dollar for the sale because the financial institution will deduct the price they received for selling the asset from the debtor.

Let's put this in terms of our example above. Two years into the loan Christian's loan defaults and his car is repossessed. He has already paid $16,200 on his loan, but much of that went to pay interest. He still owes $32,400. The car sells at auction for $15,000. So, the bank knocks $15,000 off of the remaining loan balance. This means that Christian still owes $7,400 for a car he does not own. He will receive harassing phone calls and letters and may have part of his salary taken until the loan is paid off. And while Christian pays off the loan on the car he no longer owns, how is he getting to work? Loss of job because of no transportation will force Christian to declare bankruptcy. What then?

Assuming Christian is able to pay back the full $7,400 he still owed the bank after his car was repossessed, he will have paid the bank a total of $23,600 for a $25,000 car. That makes a profit for the bank of $13,600 (minus the cost of the car and any legal or collection fees). William easily made his car payments but only paid the bank back a total of $29,000 for a $25,000 car. That makes the bank a profit of only $4,000.

The advantage to a financial institution in making a subprime loan is a greater chance for profit. The risk is if the borrower defaults on their loan and declares bankruptcy protection, then the bank may take a loss on a loan.

Risk-based pricing is the normal practice for financial institutions. Their argument is that this practice is not biased because it will still make loans to anyone who qualifies regardless of their race or sex or physical ability. The catch is "who qualifies".

When your qualifications (income) can be biased based on economic class, race, sex or physical ability then we still have a discriminatory process that relies on indirect discrimination to mask a same but unequal philosophy.

We have examined scenarios where risk-based pricing impacted the cost of a loan. In future chapters we will examine approval methodology and its' impact on denying loans. We will also explore how eliminating risk-based pricing could result in a bigger profit for banks and credit unions while reducing the financial burden on their customers.

Let's update all of our examples after they were all approved for their used car loan:

1. William is a white male that comes from a wealthy family and makes $40,000/annually. He purchased a

$25,000 car and his loan is $400/month.

2. Daniel is a white male that comes from a poor family and makes $40,000/annually. He purchased a $25,000 car and his loan is $675/month.

3. Bryan is a black male that makes $25,600/annually. He purchased a $25,000 car and his loan is $450/month.

4. Laura is female and makes $32,000/annually. She purchased a $25,000 car and her loan is $425/month.

5. Christian has autism and makes $25,200/annually. He purchased a

$25,000 car and his loan is $675/month.

These monthly loan amounts are just like our restaurant example where customers were charged different prices for their meal based on their economic class, race, sex or for being differently abled. Different prices mean's unequal treatment.

I have both professional, as well as personal, experience with subprime loans. Health issues impacted my credit which caused me to be approved for loans under a subprime rate for many years. The higher cost for my car loan and house payment made it hard to pay all of my obligations and still feed my children. I had a decent paying job, but that income was swallowed up by risk-based pricing. I had no choice but to make the car payment since no car would mean I could not make it to work and then I would have no income.

I will never forget the day I received the foreclosure notice. I will never get over the shame of seeing the red tag on my front door and on my electrical box. How do you describe to your kids that they can no longer flush the toilet? How to explain we could not turn on the lights? How do you explain they need to wrap themselves in more blankets because there would be no heat? My wife and I sacrificed, worked hard, skipped meals, and still subprime rates pushed us to near financial collapse.

An alternative to risk-based pricing will be detailed in the chapter titled Reform. But please realize these are not just hypothetical issues. An estimated 41 million people lived in poverty in 2016 in the United States (United States Census Bureau, 2017). How many of them were approved for cars and/or modest houses under a subprime rate because of factors impacted by discrimination based off of economic class, race, sex or for being differently abled? These were needed items and yet they would be overcharged for these basic necessities because of risk-based pricing.

As will be seen in a later chapter titled *Costs*, banks and credit unions could potentially make more of a profit if they do not charge risk-based prices. And yet today they are willing to carry out this discriminatory practice. For the sake of a dollar today they are willing to sacrifice two dollars tomorrow. For the sake of an immediate feast on profits they are willing to starve the most vulnerable.

Chapter 4

Credit Scores

As a person who has a deep admiration for math, the complex formula used to generate credit scores is marvelous. In my mind it ranks right up there with $E=MC^2$. Whereas Einstein was resolving the mysteries of the universe, credit score calculations allow empires to rise. In theory, they equal the playing field by allowing decisions for credit to be made regardless of economic class, race, sex or physical ability; all people are reduced only to a number. Note the "in theory" part of my comments. I will explain that shortly.

Credit scores are a numerical value assigned to an individual that shows a borrower's ability to repay a loan. That numerical value can be as low as 300 or as high as 850. In my years in banking the lowest score I personally saw was somewhere around 350. The highest score was around 800.

The factors that go into calculating your credit score are complex. A few of those are:

- If you have anything reportable. In other words, if you have no loans or lines of credit (such as a credit card), then you will have no credit score.

- Have you ever been 30, 60, or 90+ days late in making a payment on your loans or lines of credit? Being late 60 days hurts your credit score more than being late 30 days. Being late multiple times hurts your credit score more than being late only once on one loan.

- Are you in default on a loan or a line of credit?

- Were you reported for failing to pay utilities or medical bills?

- Do you have multiple lines of credit with high balances?

Based on the above criteria, a credit score is generated and a financial institution will use that score to determine if you should be approved for a loan (along with debt-to-income and loan-to-value considerations that we will discuss in future chapters) and what your interest rate should be (already discussed in the risk-based pricing chapter).

All things being equal, this is a pretty good process. However, as we have been discussing this entire book, not all things are equal. Payment history on loans, lines of credit, utilities and medical bills are impacted by your level of income as well as your economic class. And as we discussed in the chapter on income inequality, your level of income is impacted by your economic class, race, sex or physical ability.

Using credit scores to determine eligibility for a loan appears to be a non-biased way of deciding who is less of a risk and should be approved. However, when we step back and look at the bigger picture, we see that it is used as a form of indirect discrimination.

Imagine if there was a person who only slaps people with a blue dot on their hand. Now what if there was a separate person running around putting blue dots on the back of the hands of all women? Can the person who slaps everyone with a blue dot claim that they are not sexist because they only discriminate against blue dots? Likewise, can financial institutions claim they do not discriminate when their decisions are based off of discriminatory data?

What if you were a Hispanic woman making less money than a white male because of income inequality? Less income means less money to spend on your debts. Let's assume you have been responsible with your debts and were making all of your payments on time. Then the unforeseen occurred. You had a car accident and your car was totaled. As often happens, your insurance company only paid you what they considered to be the value of the car and not what you still owed on the loan. Now you have to buy another car while continuing to make payments on the loan you still have for the car you no longer own.

The extra expense stretches your income too far. The additional loan payment really makes it hard to keep the newly purchased car you must have for work. You fall behind on a couple of car payments and your credit goes from 705 before the accident down to 635 after the accident.

If you did not have to contend with income inequality and made as much money as a white male, then you would have had enough income to pay the extra expense of the new car. As it is, your lower income resulted in your credit score falling.

Say you find a way to payoff both loans through hard work and sacrifice. Your credit score was still lowered because of some late payments. Even with a new job, making $30,000 more per year in income, your lower credit score could still cause you to be approved for a house loan under a subprime rate. That will cost you thousands of dollars, possibly over $100,000 more in interest and payments because your credit score was lowered, in part, because of income inequality.

This seems like a good time to discuss the federal regulations that purport to prevent discrimination in the lending process. Those include the **Equal Credit Opportunity Act (ECOA)** and the **Fair Housing Act (FHA)** as defined by Fair Lending Laws and Regulations (FDIC, 2015).

The **Equal Credit Opportunity Act (ECOA)** forbids credit discrimination on the basis of race, color, religion, national origin, gender, marital status, age and source of income if it is through public assistance. The loan officer cannot look at you and deny your loan because you are black. They cannot deny your loan because you are a woman. However, they can deny your loan because of your credit score and we have seen already that calculation is impacted by protected reasons such as being black or being a woman. Therefore, the ECOA is too limited in its scope. Its great that lenders cannot get away with direct discrimination because of this act, but this does not prevent indirect discrimination.

The **Fair Housing Act (FHA)** prohibits the same type of discrimination as the ECOA but is focused solely on loans involving residential real-estate. Very important. Especially given the old practice of lenders "redlining" neighborhoods that they refused to lend to. But again, it too is limited in scope to cover only direct discrimination.

Neither act has yet been extended to include credit score calculations that are based in part off of income inequality. Perhaps court challenges by customers who are denied credit because of data impacted by income inequality would lead to a positive change. We will discuss that in the chapter titled Reform.

I want to add something from my own personal experience as a loan officer. Financial institutions argue that credit decisions are not made off of credit score alone. And that is somewhat true. Debt-to-income calculations, loan-to-value calculations, length of employment, length of residency all go into the decision-making process. If you had a credit score of 825 but your loan-to-value on a loan would be 150%, then you would certainly be denied. However, that only paints part of the picture.

In that scenario of a 150% loan-to-value (remember we will cover loan to value calculations in a future chapter) with an 825-credit score, if you lower the amount of the loan request so it falls under 90% loan-to-value and you have the income to support paying back the loan then you will still be approved. However, if you have a low enough credit score there is nothing you can do to be approved.

If your debt-to-income (covered in a future chapter) was 20% and your loan to value was 60% and your credit score was 425 then you will be denied. Period. No subprime loan offer will be coming in. You are out of luck. Find a co-signor with a better credit score or learn to live with disappointment.

So, I would position current bank and credit union policy as this; "You need more than a good credit score to be approved for a loan. But you only need a bad credit score to be denied".

Putting all of this together, let's apply credit score calculations to our 5 examples.

- William's credit score will be tied as the highest out of all of our examples. He has not been late on any payments because his wealthy parents were able to help him out. He did not face income inequality when compared to the other people in our examples.

- Laura's credit score is tied with William's to be the second highest. She faces a smaller wage gap than Bryan and Christian. With little debt so far, she has still been able to make her payments on time.

- Bryan likely would have the next highest credit score. As a black male Bryan faces a large wage gap that makes it harder for him to afford his debt and make all payments on time. However, so far, his parents have been able to help him financially on the rare occasion that he needed it. He is getting by, for now, with only one late payment on his car loan.

➢ Daniel would have the next to lowest credit score. Remember that he came from a poor family and fell behind on a few payments that his parents could not afford to help him pay. With little credit history these infractions were enough to make him appear to be a considerable risk. Since his income is not as impacted by income inequality,

Daniel has the chance to rebuild his credit over time. The main obstacle being how expensive his subprime loans will be until his credit is fixed.

➢ Christian would have the lowest credit score. Facing a significant wage gap and a family that could not afford to help him in his adult years, he fell behind on loan payments and eventually had his car repossessed. Struggles with transportation will make it harder for Christian to keep his job and he will most likely fall further behind on any other financial obligations.

Let's update all of our examples with their current loans and credit scores:

1. William is a white male that comes from a wealthy family and makes $40,000/annually. He purchased a $25,000 car and his loan is $400/month. His credit score is currently 720.

2. Daniel is a white male that comes from a poor family and makes $40,000/annually. He purchased a $25,000 car and his loan is $675/month. His credit score is currently 605.

3. Bryan is a black male that makes $25,600/annually. He purchased a $25,000 car and his loan is $450/month. His credit score is currently 705.

4. Laura is female and makes $32,000/annually. She purchased a $25,000 car and her loan is $425/month. Her credit score is currently 720.

5. Christian has autism and makes $25,200/annually. He purchased a $25,000 car that was repossessed after two years. In order to pay off the car he no longer owns, his current monthly payment to the bank is $100. His credit score is currently 470.

Chapter 5

DTI

DTI is an acronym for Debt-to-Income. It is calculated as a ratio of a borrower's total monthly debt (including rent) divided by the borrowers monthly gross income. When adding in the monthly payment for any new loan, a financial institution prefers to see a DTI of less than approximately 40%. The lower your DTI, the greater the chance you will be able to pay back your loan because of the extra income you make each month.

The current rationale that DTI should be below 40% rather than say 85%, is because the calculation only takes into consideration your monthly recurring debt. Your monthly minimum due on credit card debts, your monthly mortgage, your monthly car loan would all be calculated into DTI. But your utility payments, grocery bills, car insurance payment, etc. would not be. If you took out enough loans to have a DTI of 100% then you would have zero dollars to keep the lights on or take a shower or buy food. So less than 40%, by today's standard, seems reasonable.

Let's examine a DTI ratio calculation:

- Fred has an annual salary of $60,000. He has a mortgage and the monthly payment is $900. He also has a car loan for $250 per month. He has one credit card with a balance of $1,000 but a monthly minimum due of $20. He wants to take out a second car loan that would cost him an additional $300 per month.

  - With the new loan, Fred's monthly credit debt would be $1,470 ($900 + $250 + $20 + $300).

- Fred's monthly gross income is $5,000 ($60,000/12 months).

- The DTI ratio would be 29.4% ($1,470/$5,000).

    o In this example, Fred's DTI of 29.4% would be ideal for the bank. Assuming his credit score is high enough and loan-to-value is low enough (loan-to-value to be covered in another chapter), Fred would be approved for the loan. After making all loan payments, Fred would still have enough cash left over each month to easily pay for his utilities and groceries.

As we have discussed before, "all things being equal" this is a great approach. Debt-to-income ratio calculations help financial institutions determine who can afford a new loan, without apparent consideration to race, gender or physical ability. The issue again comes down to income inequality.

Since there is a wage gap based on race, sex and for those that are differently abled, then the numbers being used to make DTI ratio calculations are already discriminatory.

Let's again use the example of Fred. However, instead of using his full income let's apply a wage gap that might exist if he were differently abled. So instead of making the full $60,000 annual income let's go off of recent research and say he only makes 63% of that income. Assuming all other monthly debt information is the same, we can calculate his DTI:

- Fred has an annual salary of $37,800. He has a mortgage and the monthly payment is $900. He also has a car loan for $250 per month. He has one credit card with a balance of $1,000 but a monthly minimum due of $20. He wants to take out a second car loan that would cost him an additional $300 per month.

- With the new loan Fred's monthly credit debt would be $1,470 ($900 + $250 + $20 + $300).

- Fred's monthly gross income is $3,150 ($37,800/12 months).

- The DTI ratio would be 46.7% ($1,470/$3,150).

- In this example, Fred's DTI of 46.7% would be too high for the bank to approve his loan request. His request would be denied as high DTI. But we know the reason it was too high was because of the wage gap that prevented him from making as much money as someone who was not differently abled.

Should financial institutions have a responsibility to level the playing field for existing gaps in wages between races, genders and those that are differently abled? Should debt-to-income calculations be more inclusive of supporting criteria?

In the examples above, Fred #1 would have an extra gross income each month of $3,530 after making all loan payments. Fred #2 would only have $1,680.

But there are other things that could be considered that currently are not:

- Fred #1 would owe approximately $5,500 more per year in federal taxes than Fred #2. That money would not be discretionary.

- What if Fred #1 paid $150 more per month for a different health insurance plan than Fred #2 did?

- What if Fred #1 paid $100 per month for dental insurance and Fred #2 did not take out dental insurance?

- What if Fred #1 spent an extra $200 per month for the latest and greatest cell phone while Fred #2 only paid

$50 per month for an old flip phone and a basic plan?

- What if Fred #1 "had to have" a tv plan that allowed him to watch the big game on all 3 televisions in his home and he paid $150 per month to ensure it? Fred #2 hates television and reads everything on the shelves at his local library.

- What if Fred #1 took his wife and kids on a Disney vacation every year while Fred #2 went each year to a cabin his parents owned and he fished for a week to "recharge his batteries"?

If we consider all of these additional expenses, we would find that both Fred #1 and Fred #2 spend the same percentage of their paychecks each month. Both save about $100 a month from their income. And yet Fred #2 was denied a loan because the bank or credit union was only considering monthly credit obligations and not discretionary spending.

I understand that Fred #1 could theoretically not take his annual family vacation or could cancel his expensive tv plan. But theoretically Fred #2 could also take on a part-time job or borrow money from his parents or get a raise. Taken as a financial snapshot in time, both Fred's had the income to pay back the new loan. But only one was denied the loan because of income inequality and a short-sighted review of total monthly expenses.

Let's move away from Fred and look at more familiar examples. Let's assume our regular 5 people have all finally paid off their car loans and are now looking to buy a house. They are still single, so let's keep their income level the same. The new house will give them a monthly mortgage of $1,000. We will use the credit scores we established for them in the last chapter and we will assume loan to value is acceptable for all 5 loan requests.

1. William is a white male that comes from a wealthy family and makes $40,000/annually. His credit score is currently 720. His DTI with the new mortgage would be 30%. Credit score is very good. Loan approved.

2. Daniel is a white male that comes from a poor family and makes $40,000/annually. His credit score is currently 605. DTI is also 30% but the credit score is too low due to some late payments. Loan denied.

3. Bryan is a black male that makes $25,600/annually. His credit score is

currently 705. Credit score is good, having only had 1 late payment ever. However, because of his lower income, his DTI ratio would be 47%. Loan denied.

4. Laura is female and makes $32,000/annually. Her credit score is currently 720. Good credit score. DTI ratio would be 38%. High DTI but would most likely be approved because of her strong credit score.

5. Christian has autism and makes $25,200/annually. His credit score is currently 470. Credit score is too low. DTI ratio would be 48%, which would be too high. Loan denied.

A few things to note in the examples above.

➤ Laura was approved for the same house as William. But because of her lower income due to the wage gap of her being female, she may choose to purchase a less expensive house and keep more of her monthly paycheck for other expenses or luxuries. So, it may not be obvious, but the wage gap may still be to blame for why her future children may end up in a different part of town, in a different school system, etc.

➤ Daniel still makes as much income as William since he too is not facing the same wage gap issue. Therefore, he may choose to rent a house in the suburbs while he saves his money and rebuilds his credit. This may still allow for his future children to attend a quality school and to live in a safer area of his choosing.

➤ Bryan's income is impacted enough by the wage gap to limit some of his choices. Despite strong credit, it prevented him from buying the house he wanted. Making 64% less than his white peers also limits his other options in housing. Making only $2,133 every month before taxes, Bryan can most likely only afford to rent a cheaper place to live, such as a small house or an apartment. Often those cheaper places to live are in locations that are less safe and with poorer schools than where William moved to. His solid credit and ability to take on credit card debt will most likely save him from having to move to the same area of town as Christian.

➤ Christian's wage gap, like Bryan's, limits his housing choices. His poor credit limits his choices even more. He will most likely need to move into the cheapest place available, either with his parents (if they can afford to take him in) or in the cheapest apartment he can find in the least desirable part of town. This apartment will most likely be located in a high crime area where educational opportunities for his future children are very poor.

What does all of this mean in practical terms? 5 different individuals, working in the same industry, ended up in very different places because of institutionalized discrimination. Unfair practices around income are not being accounted for in the financial industry and this is causing very different trajectories for our citizens based on their race, their sex or their physical abilities. Bias in our credit reporting is also allowing discrimination against those whose parents are part of the economically depressed population.

Race alone is the reason Bryan is now renting a small house in a less safe part of town with less opportunities for a quality education for his children. That can be seen through the proceeding chapters as we have traced his steps. This racism contributes to why in the first quarter of 2018 black homeownership was at 42.2% and white homeownership was at 72.4% (United States Census Bureau, 2018).

His autism is the reason that Christian now lives in a cockroach infested apartment in a neighborhood that has already had 12 homicides this year. According to research, in 2016 the unemployment rate among the disabled in the United States was 64% and the percentage of the disabled population that was living below the poverty line was 21% (Kraus, Lauer, Coleman, & Houtenville, 2018). The difference in those percentages is telling as it represents the amount of additional financial assistance needed by those that are differently abled (assistance from family, government programs, or both).

The differences in their parents' income is the only difference between the house William owns and the house that Daniel is throwing his money away renting. Whereas William is building his equity, Daniel is building someone else's investment.

Gender alone is the reason Laura ended up buying a smaller house where two of her children will need to share a room.

The financial industry can claim their decisions are free from discrimination. However, they do not do anything to rectify already existing discrimination in incomes. They also compound the issues through risk-based pricing and limiting the scope of consideration around debt-to-income ratios.

Chapter 6

LTV

LTV is an acronym for Loan-to-Value. When calculated, it is a ratio that represents the percentage of an assets value that is being requested as a loan. For example, if a house's value is $100,000 and you are requesting a loan of $90,000 to purchase the house, then the LTV would be calculated as 90,000/100,000 = 90%.

The risk appetite for LTV is always changing depending on the overall economy. When deposit balances are up, financial institutions are more earnest to make loans and are therefore more willing to approve customers with a higher LTV. Leading up to the Great Recession in 2008 many financial institutions were willing to lend up to 125% LTV on houses. After the housing market collapse, credit restricted and LTV requirements fell under 100% and were typically only accepted under 90%.

Loan-to-value ratio calculations are influenced by discrimination in the loan amount being requested. This is because the LTV relates to the amount of money a potential buyer has been able to save for a down payment. And that is influenced by wage disparities that exist around economic class, race, sex, and physical ability.

In our example above, we stated that a house was valued at $100,000. Let's say the owner wanted to turn a profit when selling and the house was listed on the market at $110,000. If a potential buyer had $20,000 saved in their savings account and could use that as a down payment, then they would only need to ask a bank for a loan of $90,000. Their LTV ratio would be 90% (90,000/100,000). If their credit scores were high enough and their DTI low enough, they would most likely be approved for the loan.

What if the potential buyer did not have $20,000 set aside in a savings account and wanted to buy the same house? What if they only had $5,000 saved? Then that same potential buyer would pay $5,000 as a down payment and would need a bank loan to fund the remaining $105,000 asking price. The LTV ratio would be 105% (105,000/100,000). This customer would most likely be denied the loan because of high LTV.

The only difference in the two scenarios above is the amount of money saved by the potential buyer that can be used as a down payment for a loan. As we have stated several times before, "all things being equal" this seems like a pretty good approach to determine who should be approved and who should be denied a loan. The problem remains that not all things are equal.

Going back to the 5 examples we have been working with throughout this book, William makes $40,000 in his job in marketing. At this higher income he is able to save more each month than

Bryan. Bryan also works in the same industry but makes less money because of income inequality. Therefore, William should be able to save more for this house than Bryan and in a shorter period of time. And the reason Bryan would have the higher LTV would be because he is black.

Discrimination reflected in LTV calculations is not only the result of income inequality. Compare William to Daniel. Because Daniel's family is poor, they could not help him out when he fell behind on a couple of bills. Therefore, Daniel's credit rating fell and he has been stuck paying subprime risk prices for his loans. This has greatly reduced the amount of money Daniel can save each month even though he makes the same money as William.

Also, let's assume William hated saving money. Every month he spent every spare penny on eating out, going to sporting events, and buying whatever he wanted. When it came time to buy a house, his wealthy parents were in a better position to help him out with the purchase. Therefore, they gave William $20,000 for the down payment. Daniel could not receive the same level of help from his parents because they are poor. He could only make a $5,000 down payment that represented years of scraping and sacrifice. In this scenario, Daniel would be denied the loan, because of high LTV, because he came from an economically depressed family.

Loan-to-value ratio calculations are considered very important to a financial institution. If a customer defaulted on a $90,000 house that had a value of $100,000, the financial institution could foreclose on the house and resell it. If they were able to sell it for the full $100,000 then they could still make a profit even off of a customer's failure to pay. However, financial institutions find it difficult to make 100% of an assets value when they sell a house or a car that has been repossessed.

Maintaining empty houses is an expensive cost for a financial institution. Lawn care, routine maintenance and building security are bills no financial institution wants to take on. They would rather be in the business of collecting deposits, making loans, and making money off the interest rate difference. Also, many houses that fall into foreclosure need repairs. Those things that need to be fixed often drive down the value of the house, as well as the banks desire to sell the house quickly. Therefore, financial institution owned houses typically sell at a deep discount.

Let's look again at our 90% LTV example. Say Brenda took out the $90,000 loan on a $100,000 house and defaulted after making payments for 3 years. Assume the house did not change in value during that time period. Brenda will have paid $18,000 to the financial institution, much of that in interest for the loan. Because much of that payment only covered interest, Brenda still owes $87,000 on the loan. The bank sells the property at auction for $45,000. Brenda lives in a state that allows deficiency judgements and therefore still owes the bank $42,000 (87,000 – 45,000). She can either setup a payment plan to continue paying for a house she no longer owns or file for bankruptcy. If she does not declare bankruptcy, the bank will end up making a profit of $15,000 ($18,000 + $45,000 + $42,000 - $90,000 house value). Essentially, a small profit for the bank even if the customer defaults on the loan.

In that same scenario above, assume the LTV is 130%. Brenda takes out a $130,000 loan to purchase a house valued at $100,000. She makes payments for 3 years and loses the house through foreclosure. This time she will have paid $23,500 before losing the house. Because much of that payment only covered interest, Brenda still owes $126,000 on the loan. The bank sells the property at auction for $45,000. Brenda lives in a state that allows deficiency judgements and therefore still owes the bank $81,000 (126,000 – 45,000). She can either setup a payment plan to continue paying for a house she no longer owns or file for bankruptcy. If she does not declare bankruptcy the bank will end up making a profit of $19,500 ($23,500 + $45,000 + $81,000 - $130,000 house loan). A slightly better investment for the bank even if the customer defaults.

So, what if the Brenda's choose declaring bankruptcy versus paying off their loan balances after their homes are sold through foreclosure?

- In the 90% LTV example above, the bank will take a loss of $27,000

- In the 130% LTV example above, the bank will take a loss of $61,500

Because the higher the LTV, the greater the risk of potential loss for the bank, financial institutions have decided to only approve loans with lower LTV's. But what about the potential for gains?

In the Brenda examples, if the houses had not been foreclosed on and the loans would have gone the full 30 years, then:

- In the 90% LTV example above, the bank will make $164,000 ($74,000 that is interest rate profit) by the time the loan is paid off

- In the 130% LTV example above, the bank will make $237,000 ($107,000 that is interest rate profit) by the time the loan is paid off

Currently, only 1 in 2,058 homes are foreclosed on in the United States (RealtyTrac, (2018). If we apply that statistic to our Brenda examples above, and 2,057 of the same types of loans are fully paid off and only 1 loan is in default:

- In the 90% LTV example above, the bank will make $152,191,000 in interest rate profit
- In the 130% LTV example above, the bank will make $220,037,500 in interest rate profit

The bottom line is that if a client has a high enough credit score and a low enough debt-to-income to qualify for a loan, then the bank would profit more by approving requests than it would by declining them, regardless of LTV calculations.

Financial institutions could also do more to make it easier for buyers to afford their loans. One way to do this would be to address the discriminatory use of requiring Primary Mortgage Insurance (PMI) on all primary mortgage loans that are above 80% LTV (more on PMI in a future chapter). Financial institutions could also do more to maximize their profits on homes sold through foreclosure, rather than dumping them back on the market "as is" and leaving the former home owner with the difference in the bill.

Remembering that Daniel, Bryan and Christian have already been denied a mortgage loan for other reasons, let's examine LTV impact on our remaining two examples. The market value on the house is $140,000. The house is selling for $160,000 in a neighborhood with good schools, low crime and where houses rarely are put up for sale.

1. William is a white male that comes from a wealthy family and makes $40,000/annually. His credit score is currently 720. His DTI with the new mortgage would be below 40%. Credit score is excellent. His parents give him $20,000 and he adds another $14,000 of his own money to

make a down payment. So, the loan request would be for $126,000 (160,000 − 20,000 − 14,000). LTV would be 90% (126,000 / 140,000). Loan approved.

2. Laura is female and makes $32,000/annually. Her credit score is currently 720. Excellent credit score. DTI ratio would be below 40%. Her lower wages result in her only having $5,000 saved up for a down payment. Her mother was able to help her out with a $10,000 personal loan. So, the loan request would be for $145,000 (160,000 − 5,000 − 10,000). LTV would be 104% (145,000 / 140,000). Loan denied because of high LTV.

Again, we see that income inequality in paying different salaries based on race, gender or physical ability has resulted in applicants being treated differently based solely on a "protected" status. When financial institutions fail to account for this discrimination, they too are discriminating.

In the example above, Laura's debt to income was low enough to qualify for the mortgage and her credit score is very good. But because she is female and could not save enough due to her lower wages despite working in the same industry as William, she is unable to buy the same house. Oddly, her loan would have been more profitable to the bank and she has the income to support the payments. Yet William will be moving into the more desirable neighborhood, not Laura.

One more thing needs to be covered in a conversation about home values. Like all things in a supply and demand economy, they are based on what people are willing to pay for a house. Neighborhoods with lower crime rates and better schools are more in demand than those with higher crime and lower school test scores. Therefore, when a house goes up for sale in a neighborhood where others want to live, the seller can expect to sell it for more money, or a greater value. Conversely, a house in a high crime area with low test scores would have to sell their house at a lower percentage of the house's value in order to find an interested buyer.

An example of this would be:

> ➢ Robert wants to sell his house in an affluent neighborhood with low crime and good schools. The value of his house is $200,000. He knows he lives in a neighborhood that other families want to live in. So, he lists his house on the market for $220,000. Assuming a potential buyer puts zero dollars down for a

down payment, the LTV to purchase this house would be 110%.

> Samuel wants to sell his house in a less affluent neighborhood with higher crime rates and schools with lower test scores. The value of his house is $100,000. He knows he lives in a neighborhood that would not attract most families. So, he lists his house on the market for $80,000. Assuming a potential buyer puts zero dollars down for a down payment, the LTV to purchase this house would be 80%.

Since we have established that income inequality based on race, sex or physical ability impacts the amount of money a person can save, houses selling at a higher LTV would tend to exclude this group of buyers. Therefore, Robert will most likely sell his house to a family not impacted by income inequality, with a patriarch that makes good money. Odds are that it will be a wealthier white male. Samuel will most likely sell his house to a person or family impacted by the wage gap or by generational low income. Odds are that it will not be a wealthy white male unless they are using the house as an investment property.

Basing lending decisions and interest rates on loan-to-value ratio calculations tends to alter demographics. Those impacted by income inequality and inherited lower economic class tend to buy houses or rent apartments in the same area. It is what they can afford. Those not impacted tend to mass together as well, being able to afford to live where crime is lower and the schools are considered "superior".

Certainly, these are broad generalizations and exceptions can be found to any rule. But when we base home purchases on LTV rates knowing that LTV is impacted by discrimination through income inequality and that financial institutions are not factoring in that disparity, we see that the rules to homeownership are the "same but unequal". And neighborhoods across America, failing to reflect diversity, actually reflect financial discrimination in the lending process.

Chapter 7

PMI

PMI is an acronym for Primary Mortgage Insurance. It is associated with a mortgage's loan-to-value and involves the borrower's credit score. Since we have discussed those things in the previous chapters, now is the perfect time to discuss PMI.

When you take out a home loan for greater than 80% LTV, the lender typically requires the borrower to pay for primary mortgage insurance. This is an additional insurance policy that partially protects the lender if the borrower defaults on the house and it is foreclosed on.

The cost to the borrower for PMI could be as low as 0.25% or as high as 2% of the remaining loan balance. Many factors go into establishing the percentage a borrower would be required to pay. A few of those factors include:

- LTV (higher percentage = higher PMI percentage)

- DTI (higher percentage = higher PMI percentage)

- Credit score (lower number = higher PMI percentage)

- Loan term (15 years, 30 years, 40 years, etc.) The longer the term = higher PMI percentage

As an example, Lee just took out a loan of $180,000 for a house valued at $200,000. His LTV is 90%. His credit score is 680. His lender requires a 1% PMI policy that will cover the lender for 25% in case Lee defaults on his loan. Here is what we know about Lee's PMI policy:

- Initially, Lee will pay an additional $150 per month for his house in order to pay the PMI policy that is required by the financial institution.

- If Lee defaults on his loan, the PMI policy will pay his financial institution $45,000, reducing their losses. Lee will receive nothing despite paying for the policy himself.

- Lee will continue to make monthly payments on his PMI policy until his LTV is under 80% of the houses current value. So, if his house drops in value to only $160,000 then Lee will continue making PMI payments until his loan balance is below $128,000.

- If the house stays at a value of $200,000 and Lee makes his regular payments on time, he will end up paying approximately $10,000 on his PMI policy before it can be cancelled. If the house goes down in value, Lee could end up paying a lot more.

- None of the money spent on a primary mortgage insurance policy goes towards the overall loan balance.

We have seen in previous chapters that the income inequality between races, genders and those who are differently abled has an impact on overall credit scores and debt-to-income ratio calculations, as well as the amount a borrower may have saved in order to impact loan-to-value calculations. We have seen a similar correlation for those people who are from a family who was economically depressed.

With PMI insurance requirements we see that the same group facing income inequality are also facing higher mortgage payments. Those that made less income because of income inequality had some negative hits to their credit scores and/or had a high debt-to-income ratio and could not save enough of a down payment to avoid the 80% LTV requirement to avoid paying PMI insurance. As a result, they could end up paying thousands, or even tens of thousands of dollars more for the same house as someone not facing income inequality.

In the judicial system we have laws in place to prevent double jeopardy. This means that the same person cannot be tried twice for the same offense. Yet in our financial system we do not seem to practice double jeopardy. Good concept I guess until it interferes with the almighty dollar. Instead, we punish the poor multiple times for the "offense" of being in an ethnic minority, or for their gender, or for being differently abled or because they were raised by the poor.

- ➢ You are a black woman? Statistics say:
  - Expect lower pay than white people
  - Expect lower pay than men
  - Lower credit scores because of lower pay
  - Higher DTI because of lower pay
  - Higher LTV because of lower pay
  - Greater chance for denial of loans
  - Greater chance to live in a high crime neighborhood
  - Greater chance of living in a place with lower school test scores

- If approved to buy a house, you have a greater chance to pay subprime rates which will greatly increase your monthly payments
- If approved to buy a house, you have a greater chance to need to pay for primary mortgage insurance which will increase your monthly payments

More could be said but I am limiting my scope to financial discrimination (for this book anyway). But that alone is 10 "jeopardies" for being a black woman as it relates to finances. 10 penalties for what crime? Our diversity is God's handiwork. And God commits no crimes.

As for financial institutions, it is apparent from research report after research report that there is an income inequality in play for people of different races, different genders and for those that are differently abled. And we must not forget that we should not discriminate against someone for being poor or for being raised in a poor household. Therefore, more must be done than collect data on how many minority applicants you approved loans for or how many mortgages you granted to poor neighborhoods. We must equal the playing field through bold and innovative ideas. We will discuss this more in the chapter ahead on banking solutions.

For now, let's show the impact of primary mortgage insurance on our familiar examples. And let's assume a few things:

- All of them decided to buy a cheaper house. One valued at $100,000.

- To keep the example simple, let's assume the monthly cost for property taxes is $300. The monthly cost for homeowner's insurance is $50. Those costs will be added into the monthly payment amount for each example.

- Assume that when primary mortgage insurance is required, it is borrower paid.

- Daniel has been working hard and therefore his credit has greatly improved. It is now good enough to be approved for a mortgage loan, but he still only qualifies for a subprime interest rate.

- Christian had to move back in with his parents. It will take a lot of hard work for his credit and financial situation to recover, if it ever does. He will not be included in our mortgage examples.

1. William is a white male that comes from a wealthy family and makes $40,000/annually. His credit score is currently 720. His parents give him $12,000 for a down payment on the new house. He adds another $10,000 of his own money to the down payment. The loan is now only for $78,000 which is a loan-to-value ratio of 78%. Debt-to-income with the new mortgage would be 23%. Credit score is excellent. Loan approved. Primary mortgage insurance not required since he is below 80% loan-to-value. Total monthly payment is $750.

2. Daniel is a white male that comes from a poor family and makes $40,000/annually. His credit score is currently 665. He can put $5,000

cash as a down payment on the house. The loan will be for $95,000. Loan-to-value is 95%. Debt-to-income is 35%. Loan approved but under a subprime rate. Primary mortgage insurance is required. Total monthly payment is $1,175.

3. Bryan is a black male that makes $25,600/annually. His credit score is currently 705. Credit score is fair, having only had 1 late payment ever. He will not make a down payment on the house. Total loan will be for $100,000. Loan-to-value is 100%. Debt-to-income ratio would be 48%. Loan approved but under a subprime rate because of high LTV. Primary mortgage insurance is required. Total monthly payment is $1,175.

4. Laura is female and makes $32,000/annually. Her credit score is currently 720. Good credit score. Her mother gives her a personal loan of $5,000. Laura also adds $5,000 of her own savings and therefore makes a $10,000 down payment. Loan amount will be $90,000. Loan-to-value is 90%. Debt-to-income ratio would be 34%. Loan approved. Primary mortgage insurance required. Total monthly payment is $900.

5. Christian was left off this example. I wanted to include him but I also want these examples to be based off of historic customers I have had and realistic based on their circumstances. Christian's credit score and lower income would have,

and did in reality, make it impossible for him to be approved for a mortgage loan under the current financial snapshot.

A couple on interesting facts to note from our examples:

> ➤ All of the people in our examples work in the same industry. The differences in education and current positions are based on race, sex, being differently abled and their parents' economic class.

> ➤ Daniel and Bryan ended up with the same monthly payment, although Bryan's payment history and credit score were much better than Daniel's. Daniel was subprime because of past late payments. Bryan

was subprime because of his low income, which is a direct result of his ethnicity.

As we have discussed, primary mortgage insurance is a protection for lenders in order to be partially covered in case a borrower defaults on their loan. However, the increased expense to the borrower makes it harder for them to continue making their mortgage payments. In some instances, the extra expense of primary mortgage insurance is what causes borrowers to default on their mortgage. Sometimes it is the higher subprime rates.

Also, consider that a primary mortgage insurance policy will cause the financial institution to be less likely to work with struggling customers who are having a hard time making payments. Knowing that they will make money from the PMI policy, banks would have less reason to postpone foreclosure.

Foreclosure among those impacted by income inequality is nearly twice that of those that do not experience a significant wage gap (Bocian, Ernst, & Li, 2010). Having spent the past few chapters examining the impact of income inequality on loan decisions, interest rates and primary mortgage insurance costs, we can see why. These numbers will not equalize until financial institutions incorporate changes to their processes to ensure fairness in loan decisioning and pricing.

Chapter 8

Alternative Financing –
Payday and Title Loans

The neighborhood I grew up in has changed. It was never wealthy. We were never rich. The houses were stacked so close together that you could hear the neighbors when they cooked. My childhood was spent hopping fences and running with my friends to all of the small shops and fast food places a few blocks from home. In the summers you "window shopped" in order to get a break from the heat. Many of us had air conditioner units. Often, they were broken.

My wife now teaches a few miles from my childhood home. That means I am in the old neighborhood from time to time. And I hardly recognize it as the streets that raised me.

The old Wendy's where I used to pour M&M's into a Frosty is now a payday loan store.

The old Taco Bell, where I first tried cinnamon sticks, is now a title lending store. The old doughnut shop is now a payday loan store. Half of the businesses are boarded up and sit empty. A third of them are now gambling, payday loan, title lending or rental stores.

When traditional financial institutions fail to account for income inequality, payday and title lending stores gladly step in. As a community's residents become more desperate, they become more willing to take out any loan, at any price. What are they so desperate to purchase as to turn to a payday or title lender? Food, shelter, warmth…the basic necessities that God gives freely but which mankind has slapped a price tag on. And the price to be paid for a payday or title loan, through one of these stores, is mind boggling.

Imagine that your house just burned down. What next? You call your insurance company and find out they were a fraudulent company. You have no coverage. You have to figure out where to live, what to eat, what to wear, how to get to work (your only car was in the garage at the time of the fire and it burned up as well), how to get your kids to school. You turn to your family. They do not have much but they share what they can. Your spouse and kids can sleep in your extended family's basement for a while. They can wear some of their ill-fitting, used clothes. It is embarrassing, but at least it is shelter and cover. But you still need food (they do not have enough for so many extra mouths) and you need transportation or you will lose your job. If you lose your job then you lose the only chance you have to pull yourself out of this mess. So, you weigh your options for a small, short term loan to pay for food and a bus pass. In this example we will define the cost as the number of days of your life you lose by taking a loan.

> Option 1 - If a bank provides you the small loan, through traditional

financing, then you only owe them 10 days of your life.

➢ Option 2 - If a bank provides you the small loan, through subprime lending, then you owe them 30 days of your life.

➢ Option 3 - If a payday or title lending store offers the small loan then you owe them 300 days of your life.

Out of the three options listed above I would hope all of us would choose option #1. However, as we have seen in this book already, option 1 is hard to be approved for if you are from a depressed economic class, are of a minority race, are female or are differently abled. What then? Your need is so great that you have to have the money at any cost. Your only option may very well be #3.

Payday and title loan stores use different collateral sources to approve your loan request. A payday loan is essentially a company willing to trade your next paycheck for cash today. A title loan is willing to hold the title to your car until you pay back the loan (they will then keep your car if you cannot pay back the loan). A payday loan is typically for a much smaller amount ($500 or less) than a title loan (up to $10,000 or more).

Both payday and title lenders share some dangerous features to the loans they make:

- Short term loans (have to be paid back in less than 1 month – even shorter timeframe for payday loans)

- Expensive fees

- High interest rates (if annualized the annual yield on the rates can be as high as 400% with fee costs included in the calculation)

- No consideration is given to if the customer is able to afford the new debt

For some people, payday and title lending stores are the last stop to financial ruin. For others, they are a way of life. Is it better to let your family starve or take out a high cost payday loan? Is it better to freeze to death in the winter when your heat is shutoff or to take out a title loan? When I taught business finance classes, I told my students that their first priority was to provide for the needs of their family. And I reassert that now. A payday or title loan is better than death. However, not needing one is better yet.

One more example to better understand the full impact of the high cost of expensive fees and high interest rates. Let's examine if you took out a 30-day title loan for $5,000 to pay for a new roof on the house and remediate mold in the walls that was harming your children's health. You were already living paycheck by paycheck. It will be difficult to save enough money to pay off the loan. So, the title lender is kind enough to keep rolling your debt over month after month until you pay it back. Let's assume it has been 6 months since you took out the loan:

- You could end up paying approximately $15,000 back for the $5,000 loan, after only 6 months.

- Since you are living paycheck by paycheck you will most likely never be able to pay back the full loan amount. The title loan company will end up keeping your car. Good luck on getting to work now.

- The title loan company didn't mind making the loan. If you paid it back then they would make money. If you did not then they will sell your car and make their money back that way. It is a win-win scenario for them.

- If you can pay back the loan it will cost you significant future income. If you cannot pay back the loan then it will cost you your car and possibly your job. It is a lose-lose for you.

When unemployment rises in a city, when foreclosures are increasing, when businesses are moving out of the area and plywood is being fitted over the windows, that is when you see the payday and title loan stores moving in. Where an economy is dying, they appear. Lending stores are the buzzards feeding off of the dying carcass.

In theory, there are laws about predatory loans. One definition of predatory loans are those loans that impose unfair terms on the borrower that they cannot afford. But how can we define unfair? How do we calculate "cannot afford" if these lenders do not have to calculate debt-to-income ratios? It is left up to interpretation. It is subjective. Most agree that high interest rates and fees would be unfair to those without much income. But what interest rate is defined as too high? How costly do the fees have to be to be considered unfair?

It is this subjectivity that allows payday and title lenders to continue to legally operate. And perhaps that is best until we fix the current discriminatory practices in traditional banking and address income inequality in our country. As I stated before, a bad option is better than no option and high interest rates are better than no food. But I consider it as a crime against humanity that people would seek to benefit financially from desperation. If payday and title lenders are allowed to legally operate, then there should be lower limits set on the amount of interest and fees they can charge. For once people turn to payday and title loans as a last resort, they often get buried in so much debt that they can never escape.

For their part, payday and title lenders claim that they do not make enough of a profit to be considered predatory. My response:

- Even skinny sharks are considered predators

- "Enough Profit" is still too subjective for it to define if something is predatory

- Most borrowers pay more in fees (including interest owed) than they originally received in credit (Bourke, 2016).

> Payday and title loans combine as a multibillion-dollar annual industry. Hard to logically conclude that is not "enough profit"

How does a discussion about payday and title lending stores fit into a book about financial discrimination? I will answer that with other questions. How many wealthy people take out payday and title loans? How many middle-class bread winners take out payday and title loans?

These high interest loans are reserved for those who are poor or are on their way to being poor. It is for those most impacted by generational, depressed economic status or those facing income inequality due to racism, sexism and ableism. When banks and credit unions fail to negate the impact of income inequality and then amplify its damaging effects through additional financial discrimination, then payday and title loan stores take advantage and turn a high profit at the expense of those already living on borrowed resources. Consider it indirect, indirect discrimination.

When working as a branch manager over multiple facilities, one of the retail stores I managed was in the economically depressed area of my childhood. Some of my customers were also customers of the local payday and title lending stores. Reviewing their paperwork, trying to find a way our bank could help them out of their debt trap, was always an emotionally painful experience. And often we could not.

What I learned from my customers was that many of them considered payday or title lenders as part of their plan to pay their ongoing monthly bills. They did not just turn to them in an "emergency" situation. Their income was low enough, and they were desperate enough, that these loans were just something they felt they needed to do in order to keep food on the table and shoes on their kid's feet.

Their lives were the emergency that needed financing.

Turning back to our 5 friends, Christian and Daniel are the most likely people to turn to a payday or title loan. Bryan is the next likely. Laura unlikely. William is the least likely to ever have the need to pay the high fees and interest rates demanded of a payroll or title loan.

1. William is a white male that comes from a wealthy family and makes $40,000/annually. His credit score is currently 720. He has few loans and those have low interest rates and monthly payments. If he has a financial emergency and becomes desperate, he can turn to his wealthy parents for assistance rather than a payday or title loan store.

2. Daniel is a white male that comes from a poor family and makes $40,000/annually. His credit score is currently 665. He has few loans but they were priced as subprime, meaning he is paying a large percentage of his monthly income towards his debts. If he has a financial emergency and becomes desperate, he cannot rely on his poor parents to provide financial assistance. With high DTI, he will not qualify for any future bank loans until his current loans are paid off. Hoping his situation is only temporary, Daniel may turn to a payday or title loan to pay a few monthly bills.

3. Bryan is a black male that makes $25,600/annually. His credit score is currently 705. Credit score is good, having only had 1 late payment ever.

Good credit but his high DTI, due to income inequality, would prevent him from being approved for another bank loan until his current loans are paid off. Like Daniel, he may turn to a payday or title loan store for assistance. However, his parents make better money than Daniel's parents, and therefore they may be able to provide enough financial assistance to help Bryan get back on his feet.

4. Laura is female and makes $32,000/annually. Her credit score is currently 720. Excellent credit score. Higher DTI than William but can still qualify for a small traditional loan through a bank. Her mother makes middle class income and can also help her out financially if necessary. Laura is unlikely to need a payday or title loan.

5. Christian has autism and makes $25,200/annually. His credit score is currently 470. Credit score is too low. Could not take out a loan with a bank even under a subprime rate. Since his parents cannot support him financially, Christian would be very likely to apply for a payroll or title loan. His lower salary, due to income inequality, would likely make him a recurring payroll and/or title loan customer.

If you do not qualify for a traditional loan with a bank or credit union, then you may be approved for what you need under a subprime rate. If you do not qualify for approval under a subprime rate, you may turn to payday or title loan stores for the cash you need. Where do you go when you can no longer qualify for a payday or title loan because you already owe them so much?

After you have cut out all personal discretionary spending (money spent on non-essential items), sold everything of monetary value and can no longer beg, plead, or borrow…what then?

Chapter 9

Bank Fees

Once upon a time...banks were established to make money through the interest rate spread. That spread is the difference between what banks pay out for deposits versus what they collect in interest for making a loan. For example, if a bank pays you 1% in interest for keeping $50,000 in a savings account and then loans that money to another customer for a loan at 5% interest, then they make their money off of the 4% difference. All of a bank's cost for operations (building and utility expense, payroll to employees, etc.) and profitability could be derived from the interest rate spread.

In my early days of banking, collecting deposits and making loans was the theme of each work day. In the morning you assembled a list of bank customers who carried larger balances in their Certificates of Deposit (CD's). During the day, between customers that came into the branch, you called your list of CD customers to inquire if they had deposits at other banks and if so, you offered them a special interest rate to move the money to you. The next day you would compile a list of customers who had equity built up in their homes and you would spend the day calling them to try to explain the benefits of establishing a home equity loan.

In the early days of my banking career, fees charged by banks provided a meager source of profit. They were mentioned in afterthought. They were not part of the overall retail strategy that was discussed and executed within the bank branches. That has since changed.

In an effort to become more and more profitable, banks have turned to fee revenue as part of their overall profitability strategy. Amounts vary by institution, but some examples of fees charged are:

- $35 charged per overdraft
- $5 charged daily for being in a negative balance

- $4 for using a different bank's ATM for a cash withdrawal
- $20 wire transfer fee
- $15 per month for a banking service
- $12 per month for a certain type of account
- $250 to establish a home equity loan
And the list goes on…

It has become such a vital part of bank strategy on profitability, that fee revenue is now counted on for providing banks billions of dollars in additional income every year. In my last job I worked for one of the largest banks in the world. We met each quarter and reviewed profitability. Fee revenue was always a part of that review and it always seemed to increase quarter after quarter, year after year.

Why do bank fees matter when discussing financial discrimination? Because fees are disproportionately charged to those impacted by income inequality.

Who would be more likely to pay an overdraft fee? Would it be the person making $60,000 per year who can check their balance every hour on their latest smartphone with 5G technology? Or would it be the person making minimum wage that cannot even afford a home computer?

Who would be more likely to carry the required minimum balance to have the monthly $12 service fee waived on their checking account? Would it be the person who is paying low interest rates on their loans because of low DTI and LTV and credit scores? Or would it be the subprime customer who is being charged hundreds of dollars extra each month for the same debt?

If you are unsure of the answer to the questions above, then let me tell you about "Fee

Friday". When I worked as the branch manager of a local bank, I noticed a trend every Friday and hence the reason I nicknamed the day. Beginning as soon as the branch opened in the morning and continuing throughout the day, people lined up outside of my office on Friday's to negotiate the fees charged to their accounts.

On Fee Friday I would meet with customers who had been assessed hundreds, sometimes thousands of dollars in fees. The first fees could have been anything…did not meet the minimum balance requirement for their account, overdrew their account because they made an adding error in their checkbook, did not realize a different bank would charge an additional fee when they used their ATM, etc. For these customers, living paycheck by paycheck, these unexpected fees often brought their already low balances into negative territory. And once that happened, they started getting charged daily fees for having a negative balance. They could not bring their balance into the positive until their next payday. For many of them that was Friday.

So, every Friday I sat with desperate customer after desperate customer. Many of them pleading, some crying, some shaking with rage, as we negotiated their debt. Since many of them lived paycheck by paycheck, every penny that was not refunded was money they could not spend on food or bills. And I was not allowed to refund all charges. Rather the strategy was to refund one or two fees and make it clear we were doing them a favor they did not deserve. We also had to make it clear we would not refund their fees again in the future. This allows financial institutions to try and shine up their image while taking money right out of their customers pockets.

What did every one of these customers have in common? Some were white, some black, some Hispanic, some were men, some were women. But all of them were children of God whose low income did not insulate them from greed.

I was coached at multiple banks that an ideal customer is someone who overdrafts their account several times a year but always pays the fees that are charged. In other terms, the working poor who felt a moral obligation to pay what they owe.

For their part, banks get creative on how and when fees are charged. And I worked for different banks that had different philosophies. For instance, if a bank receives 5 checks in one day what is the order they apply them against your account? It makes a big difference. Here are two different approaches that result in a different amount of fees being assessed:

In the first approach, the bank will apply checks against Tracey's account in the order of smallest check to largest. Tracey wrote all 5 checks. The largest check, for $150, was written two months ago and Tracey forgot that it had not yet been debited from her account. We are tracking each check as it clears the account and the remaining balance afterwards.

Check amount	Remaining Balance
$3.00	$120.00
$5.50	$114.50
$8.00	$106.50
$25.00	$81.50
$150.00	($68.50)

In this example, Tracey would be charged one $35 overdraft fee for the $150 check that overdrew her account.

Now let's take the same Tracey example and make only one small change. Let's say Tracey's bank's policy is to apply checks from largest amount to smallest.

Check amount	Remaining Balance
$150.00	($27.00)

$25.00	($52.00)
$8.00	($60.00)
$5.50	($65.50)
$3.00	($68.50)

In this example, Tracey would be charged $35 overdraft fees for all 5 checks. That would total $175 in fees.

These two different approaches resulted in a difference of Tracey #2 being charged an additional $140 in fees. Both approaches are legal. Both approaches are defended by the banks.

Fees have to be disclosed at the time of account opening and therefore banks justify charging high cost fees as being in a customers control. However, there are a few issues with this strategy:

> ➤ Fee disclosures are confusing for customers with a limited

understanding of banking and finance.

➢ Fees can be unavoidable at times for the lowest wage earners in our economy (those same wage earners more likely to be impacted by income inequality).

➢ Fees are typically waived for the higher wage earners in our economy (those same wage earners less likely to be impacted by income inequality). Not just case by case waivers, but rather entire systemic service plans and policies to not charge fees to clients with higher deposit balances. This causes a disparity in how "protected groups" are being treated at financial institutions. More on this approach in a minute.

Just like we reviewed in our discussions about loans, banks are not doing enough to account for income inequality as it impacts different races, genders, those that are differently abled and those from a lower economic class. Instead, much like risk-based pricing of loan interest rates, banks are charging a different price for overall banking to those impacted by income inequality versus those that are not.

Fee revenue has become such a lucrative business strategy for banks that it is now being leveraged to grow their deposit and loan portfolios. An example of this is a small business strategy I helped develop monitoring for at the most recent bank I worked at. It mirrored a strategy already in place for consumer customers at the bank. So, it will now impact every customer at one of the largest banks in the world.

The strategy is the latest trend in banking. Offer additional incentives to those with the highest balances at the bank. Those incentives can include discounted loan rates, cash back on credit card use, refunding of third-party fees (such as the fee another bank charges for using their ATM machine), and a waiver of any future fees.

What could a bank have to gain by waiving fees and lowering interest rates? They are looking to earn more customer business and therefore increase the amount of money they have on deposit and the amount of loans they are making, resulting in increased revenue.

As we have stated several times in this book before, "all things being equal" this sounds like a good strategy. However, we know that not all things are equal.

- ✓ Since women are making less money than men…

- ✓ Since certain races are making less money than other races…

- ✓ Since people who are differently abled are making less money than those who are not…

- ✓ Since people who were raised in low income homes typically have less money saved due to higher interest rates on loans…

   …for those reasons, all things are not equal. A rewards program that disproportionally benefits those not impacted by income inequality only adds to the financial discrimination that exists today in our financial institutions.

I understand that banks are a for-profit industry. I am a capitalist that believes that there must be an incentive for hard work and hard work grows an economy. I also believe that we need banks to be profitable in order to allow access to the financial services and loans that we all require. However, I also believe that our economy and society grow's best when we grow together. By practicing financial discrimination, banks are unfairly deciding who has the better chance at grasping the American dream.

For many, financial institutions have contributed to that dream becoming a nightmare. Banks collect billions of dollars in profit each year from their fees alone. Every dollar spent in fees is a dollar not spent on food, shelter, or an education.

- ➤ In 2016, an estimated 41 million people lived in poverty in the United States (United States Census Bureau, 2017).

- In 2016, FDIC insured banks reported net income of $171 billion (FDIC, 2018). They were even more profitable in 2017.

I ask banks to make a profit, not a killing; to make a profit fairly and not through discriminatory practices. And as will be discussed in the upcoming chapters, banks could increase their profitability by implementing fair practices. It just requires bold leadership.

Chapter 10

Costs

There are costs to denying loans. There is a cost for a bank to charge fees. There is a price to pay for financial discrimination. Some of these costs are more obvious than others. Poverty, addiction, suicide, crime have all been linked to income and finances in past research reports. Since those areas are explored in depth in other publications, I will not attempt to mimic their work here. Rather I will examine three costs that do not receive as much attention:

- ➢ The cost to financial institutions
- ➢ The cost to our overall economy
- ➢ The hidden cost

The Cost to Financial Institutions

As I explained very early in this book, I love math. So, let's try and calculate the cost to a bank for practicing financial discrimination. We will use Daniel to weigh the cost of discriminating against someone who comes from a low-income family.

Remember that Daniel's parents were poor and could not help him financially when he moved out as an adult. Because of that he was late on a couple of utility payments. This led to him being approved for a car under a subprime rate. The higher payments under the subprime rate caused him to be denied for a home loan because of a high debt-to-income ratio. Let's also assume that Daniel is charged $200 in fees per year in order to account for the fee revenue that banks currently collect.

We will look at two examples. The first example examines the profit to a bank during a 6-year span by operating under their current model of risk-based pricing.

➢ Daniel took out a 72-month auto loan that was approved under a subprime rate. Total interest paid to the bank over 6 years = $19,800.

- During 6 years Daniel paid a total of $1,200 in bank fees ($200 per year times 6 years).

- Daniel was unable to purchase a house during that 6-year time frame because of high DTI that resulted from his high interest rate under risk-based pricing.

    o Total profit to the bank over 6 years = $21,000.

For our second example under Daniel, we will eliminate risk-based pricing and all bank fees. For this example, Daniel's loan approvals will be under the same interest rate that William was approved for.

- ➤ Daniel took out a 72-month auto loan that was approved under a standard rate. Total interest paid to the bank over 6 years = $4,000.

  - During 6 years Daniel was charged no bank fees.

  - Daniel was approved to buy a house at the same time he purchased his car. Same $160,000 house as William's example, same loan interest rate. Total interest paid to the bank over 6 years = $41,000.

    - o Total profit to the bank over 6 years = $45,000.

Having Daniel pay higher rates based on risk-based pricing and making him pay bank fees looks good on paper as it relates to bank profitability. However, by charging him the same loan rate as William and by not charging him any fees, the bank was able to make an additional $24,000 in profit off of Daniel's banking relationship in just the first 6 years.

The concept for profitability is very simple. Those with more money are able to purchase more things. More purchases (i.e. cars, houses, college educations, second houses, etc.) means more loans. More loans equal more profitability from the interest rate spread.

Let's look at this concept through a different lens. There was a mall in my home town. Growing up, like most of my generation, I wandered around the mall as often as possible. There were two movie theaters inside, an arcade, multiple places to eat and it was swarming with cute girls. What a way to spend a Saturday!

By the time I was a young man the mall had already begun to change. The movie theaters had closed and some of the other stores followed them out of the building. Less people were wandering the stores. But I saw this as an opportunity to open a business and draw the crowds back in. I did my research and was prepared to open an internet café at a time when they were just coming into fashion.

To open my new café, I reached out to the manager of the mall to inquire about renting one of their empty units. What I learned stopped me dead in my tracks. They were going to charge me $2,000 a month to lease a small store front unit. This price might have made sense if it was the only unit available. However, they had several units sitting empty and the number of people visiting the mall had dropped in recent years. I weighed my options and decided that the cost was too steep when compared to the waning customer base.

Over the next few years, I visited that mall often and watched store after store close. No other businesses moved in to take their place. I spoke with store owners when they would post liquidation sales and they all said the same thing. The reason they were leaving the mall was because the monthly lease on their unit was too high for the small number of customers who still ventured inside.

We can take this real-life example and apply it back to our concept about banking profitability. Let's say the mall had a total of 100 units within the building. Just as I witnessed in reality, the more expensive the monthly rent, the less people are willing to rent the units.

- At $2,000 a month, if 40 units were rented out = $80,000 rent collected monthly.

- At $1,250 a month, if 80 units were rented = $100,000 rent collected monthly.

In this mall example we see that by charging less money for the monthly rent the mall was able to rent out more locations and therefore made $20,000 more per month in income. What they lost in per unit profit, they more than made up for by selling more.

Also, more stores rented out meant more options for customers. This should have drawn in larger crowds of shoppers. The increased number of shoppers would have attracted more businesses. As the number of units to rent became scarce, the mall owner could have raised prices to rent. Success breeds success.

As it relates to banks, the more loans made, the greater the profits. Therefore, the more banks can do to make loans affordable and fair, the greater potential profit for their organization. Another win-win.

Lawsuits and fines are another cost to financial institutions for engaging in discrimination.

Over the past decade, banks have been forced to pay billions of dollars in fines and lawsuits over accusations of discriminatory practices. This eats into profitability and makes risk-based pricing and lending decisions and fee charges even more illogical.

Since banks can make more of a profit and they can keep more of their profit by not having to pay fines and settlements, it makes more sense (and cents) to take active measures to eliminate current financially discriminatory practices.

The Cost to Our Overall Economy

What is the impact to an economy when customers are charged a higher interest rate for their bank loans in order to purchase a car or house? Gross Domestic Product growth is limited and, along with it, the overall profitability of every business. Let's look to Daniel again as an example of this concept:

- Daniel was charged a subprime rate on his car and that caused him to be declined for a house.
- Daniel ended up having to rent an existing house rather than having a new house built.

    - Let's say it takes 50 people to plan, build and sell the new house. That is 50 people who did not receive the job of building Daniel's house.
    - Those 50 people who were never hired to build Daniel's house didn't make say $100,000 for building it.
    - Let's say all 50 people would have used that money to purchase furniture for their houses (kitchen tables, couches, desks, etc.)

- Because those 50 people did not have the $100,000 in income, the house furniture was never purchased and the stores have $100,000 less.
- The stores that did not sell the $100,000 in furniture are unable to turn a profit. They are forced to close and lay off their workers. 15 people lose their jobs. That is 15 more people who are unable to buy cars, houses, furniture.
- The industries tied to the furniture stores then have less profit, etc., etc., etc.

Even as Donne wrote that "No (wo)man is an island...", even so every business is tied to every other business. What happens to company A will be felt by company B. What happens to company B will be felt by company C. So, on and so on. By charging Daniel more for the same loan as William, the bank not only lowered their own profitability, but they also lowered the profits for other businesses. This has a real impact on jobs and overall economic growth.

As in the example of overcharging Daniel for his subprime car loan, underpaying Bryan because of his race also impacts the overall economy.

Just like risk-based pricing and fee charges for banks, income inequality might look good on a balance sheet. It keeps payroll expenses down which minimizes their impact on profitability. This rings true for every business, regardless of the industry.

Since lower wages are paid to people depending on their race or gender or if they are differently abled, hiring a few workers from this group increases profits while allowing a company to meet diversity hiring requirements.

What is the impact to an economy when wages are suppressed? It is similar to our example of Daniel above.

- ➢ Bryan makes 37% less than Daniel because of income inequality.
- • Because of his lower salary, like Daniel, Bryan cannot afford to have his own house built.
    - o This means that the same group of 50 people who were not hired to build the house Daniel could not afford will also not be hired to build Bryan's new house.
    - o The company that builds houses has not had work for a couple of months. All of their potential customers are either underpaid or overcharged for their loans. This means they have to cut back on their expenses. They decide to cancel their marketing strategy and focus on cheaper word of mouth advertisement.

- Bryan and Daniel's company handled marketing for the house building company. They just lost one of their best customers. The marketing company saved $14,400 per year by paying Bryan 37% less than Daniel. And the strategy just cost them a $50,000 per year account.
- The CEO for the marketing company was just fired in favor of hiring someone who can "turn things around".

When a greater percentage of the population is making a fair wage, consumer spending goes up. Increased consumer spending means increased profitability for all businesses as well as banks who are supplying the loans to make big ticket purchases (i.e. cars and houses and business startups). When businesses are making a strong profit year over year, then they expand and hire more workers. This leads to a higher percentage of employment and increased consumer spending. This causes our economy to grow even bigger and more successful.

For those that would argue paying everyone the same would be socialism, you miss the point. Pay differences can still exist based on performance. Those pay differences would still create an environment of opportunity in a market that rewards hard work and innovation. But when you hide behind these cloaks in order to practice racism, sexism and ableism you limit the growth potential and profitability of your own business and the country you intend to pass along to your children and grandchildren.

For those that argue paying a percentage of the workforce more will result in increased inflation, you fail to understand the role of the Federal Reserve Bank on our finances. They have several tools to control the rate of inflation. Their monetary policies are complex and broad enough to account for an end to financial discrimination.

The Hidden Cost

There is a hidden cost for financial discrimination. A price all of us are forced to pay and yet can only be viewed in the abstract. The cost is the loss of potential. Not only loss of income and business growth potential, but also what could have been in a much larger context.

People make life decisions off of their finances. Your level of income and surplus savings impacts your decision to buy a house or a car, but it also impacts how many children you have, if you go to college, who you marry, if you start a business, etc.

Take Laura for example. Because of the lower income she received because of income inequality related to her gender, she had to buy a smaller house than William did. The smaller house had less bedrooms. Therefore, she may have decided it best to have less children. What if Laura only had two kids instead of three? Let's name the third child who was never given life. We will name her Grace.

What would Grace have become? What if she would have had her mother's intelligence and her father's stubbornness? A health issue she experienced in her youth caused her to be fascinated by medicine and empathetic for anyone struggling with sickness. This motivated her to learn as much as she could in college. While everyone else was out partying, she was up late each night studying. She went into the field of medical research out of college and spent two decades splicing genes and testing theories.

Finally, Grace had a breakthrough. She discovered a way to prevent genes from mutating after birth. With a single shot, a newborn baby could be prevented from ever developing cancer!

What about Bryan? Because of his lower income, based on his race, Bryan had to pay subprime rates on his loans. This prevented him from being able to afford to live in a neighborhood with better schools. His son, Warren, scored in the lowest 30% of the nation in high school test scores partly because of the poor schools he attended. His low-test scores and his parents limited income prevented him from going to college.

Warren could have been a scientist. He could have been working on disabling nuclear weapons through radio waves rather than working on an assembly line. He still grew up to be a fine young man. But the process he would have developed to disable nuclear devices was not invented in time to prevent 325 million people from dying in a global nuclear holocaust.

Dramatic examples. I agree. But the truth is, we don't know what we don't know.

We could speculate about all 5 of our examples and the impact of the decisions they made in life that were impacted by financial discrimination. Sadly, all that it can ever be is speculation. If people are prevented from reaching their full potential, we will never know what could have been.

Based on current data, if banks lowered their fees by only 10% and if that money was instead spent on high school graduates, we could afford to pay for 300,000 people to get their 4-year degree from college. Every year we could pay for another 300,000 students to get their college degree and the banks would still make over $150,000,000,000 in net profit according to 2016 numbers. How far could our technology and science and arts and knowledge advance with 300,000 more college graduates every year? In 20 years, we would have an army of 6 million more college graduates that would advance us all into the future, regardless of race or gender or physical ability. And all it takes is a little fairness in how banks are charging their fees and interest rates. A little change in interest rates and fees, compounded over millions of individuals and over time, will change the world!

    I have said it before and I will now say it again. We grow best when we grow together.

Chapter 11

Reform

Financial discrimination based on economic class, race, sex or physical ability must come to an end. It is limiting the growth potential of our businesses and the ability of the citizens of the United States to "pursue a life of Happiness".

Income inequality must be relegated to the history books. It must become part of our past that we remember with shame. There must be equal pay for equal work based on equal qualifications and equal opportunities. This will benefit citizens by allowing them equal access to the American dream. Ending income inequality will benefit businesses by increasing the number of consumers that can afford their goods or services.

While businesses effort ending income inequality, I am calling on financial institutions to voluntarily change their practices in order to eliminate the destructive impact of financial discrimination on our citizenry and economy. Those changes (with a more detailed explanation to follow) include:

1. Eliminate risk-based pricing.

2. Minimum credit scores for loan approval should be adjusted to account for income inequality.

3. Debt-to-income ratio calculations should include all of an applicant's monthly expenses.

4. Eliminate loan-to-value calculations as a basis for approving/denying loans.

5. Eliminate borrower paid Primary Mortgage Insurance requirements.

6. Payday and title loan stores should be required to perform debt-to-income ratio calculations to ensure an applicant can afford the payments on their new loan.

7. Payday and title loan stores should have their maximum interest rates and fees capped.

8. Eliminate bank fees.

9. Eliminate bank programs that offer special deposit rates and loan rate discounts to their wealthiest customers.

Eliminate risk-based pricing

Charging different prices for the same goods or services relies on discrimination. That cannot be denied. Making pricing decisions based on factors that can be impacted by economic class, race, gender or for being differently abled makes the process a form of indirect discrimination.

As we reviewed in the chapter by the same name, income inequality does impact risk-based pricing. Being raised by low-income parent(s) also impacts risk-based pricing. For this reason, charging different prices for two different individuals to receive the same loan to buy the same valued asset is simply a war on the poor.

Risk-based pricing makes it more expensive for those with less income to purchase the same assets as those with middle or upper income. And because it makes payments higher for some, it reduces the amount of goods and services that are purchased and financed. This has a negative impact on our national economy as well as the profitability of banks and credit unions, as well as all other businesses. This pricing methodology must be stopped.

Minimum credit scores for loan approval should be adjusted to account for income inequality

In a previous chapter, we examined how income inequality has an impact on overall credit scores. When someone is paid less because of their race, gender or for being differently abled then their credit score will most likely be reduced as well. For this reason, credit score minimums must be adjusted to account for income inequality.

For example, since black people make 36% less than white people on average, the minimum credit score for black people to be approved for a loan should be reduced by 36%. If the minimum credit score for approval for a white male is 680:

- ➤ Then for black people it should only be 435

➢ For women the score would be adjusted to 544
➢ For those that are differently abled the minimum score for approval should be adjusted to 428

➢ For Asian's the credit score for approval would actually need to be higher since census data indicates that Asians make about 131% more than whites, on average (Senega, Fontenot, & Kollar, 2017). Therefore, their credit score for approval should be at least 890 (which is impossible since credit scores only go as high as 850).

This strategy really gets complicated when someone fits into multiple categories. What if someone is differently abled and a woman? What credit score would be the minimum requirement for a black woman or an Asian-American man who lost his arm fighting for our country as a Marine?

I am sure this strategy sounds insane to most people. It sounds completely racist and sexist and ableist to change the measurements based on race or gender or for being differently abled. I can hear the uproar now, the names I am about to be called.

Redirect your righteous indignation. This racist, sexist and ableist behavior is already taking place every day in businesses all across America as evidenced by income inequality. Once we solve income inequality then we do not need a sliding measure when it comes to credit scores. However, without equal pay we cannot have equal measurements.

I challenge banks and other financial institutions to find a better solution when it comes to considering credit scores for loan decisions. A solution that negates the impact of income inequality on credit.

Debt-to-income ratio calculations should include all of an applicant's monthly expenses

Debt-to-income ratio calculations are also impacted by income inequality and therefore racist, sexist and ableist factors. When people receive less income, their debt-to-income ratios will be higher. That is simply a mathematical fact. Not an "alternative fact". Not a "speak your truth" kind of fact. Not a "leftist liberal" fact. Not a "conservative right" fact. Not a "Democratic" or "Republican" fact. And that is why I love math. $2 + 2 = 4$ without prejudice.

If you make $4,000 in income monthly and have $1,000 a month due in loans, then your debt-to-income ratio is 25%. If you make $5,000 monthly and you have the same $1,000 due monthly, then your debt-to-income ratio is 20%. More income means lower DTI and an easier chance for a loan approval. Fact!

Since debt-to-income can be impacted by discriminatory factors through income inequality and through risk-based pricing, it must be more comprehensibly reviewed.

Currently, only monthly loans, lines of credit payments and rent are calculated into the ratio. But this does not take into consideration an applicant's lifestyle. A lower-income conservative person with a higher DTI will be able to make their loan and rent payments easier than a middle-income individual that buys large quantities of penny stocks every month in the hope of hitting it big. Therefore, raising the DTI limit for approvals, with an emphasis on learning a customers full spending habits, will make DTI calculations fairer across the board. They will not solve for income inequality but they will move the lending decision process in the direction of equality.

I am sure the banks are now saying that loans and rent are something we can easily prove the customer owes. They could lie to us about the dollar amounts that they spend on utilities and groceries and entertainment, etc. True, they could lie. That is why you do not make a credit decision based solely on debt-to-income ratios. You review the customers credit report and see if they have ever defaulted on a past loan. If they have a history of paying their loans and those payments were mostly on time, then they have earned the benefit of the doubt. They should be trusted to make their payments on the new loan. Again, DTI still needs to be established below 100%. I would even argue 80% or lower. We all need a buffer in case of emergency. But by approving only requests with 40% or lower DTI and limiting our scope to only loans and rent for consideration, banks and credit unions are allowing income inequality to play an outsized role in the lending process by not reviewing the whole person and their full financial habits.

Eliminate loan-to-value calculations as a basis for approving/denying loans

As was discussed in the chapter on loan-to-value calculations, LTV ratios can be impacted by financial discrimination as it relates to asset value and the amount of money a borrower is able to save for a down payment. Therefore, basing credit decisions off of an assets value and a customer's down payment amount, propagates further discrimination and can prevent loans, and therefore purchases, by individuals because of their race, sex or for being differently abled.

If an applicant has a proven credit history of loan repayments and the new loan they are applying for will still cause them to have a low enough debt-to-income ratio, then they should be approved for a loan regardless of an assets value.

DTI limitations will still prevent the loan from being approved under an exaggerated amount (i.e. a $400,000 loan to buy a $100,000 house). Eliminating risk-based pricing and borrower paid primary mortgage insurance will make the monthly payments more affordable. Credit history will still show who has been paying their loans responsibly. All of these factors should be sufficient to limit risk for the financial institution in deciding the loan request.

Eliminate borrower paid Primary Mortgage Insurance requirements

The amount of money that can be deposited when buying a new house is influenced by discriminatory factors involving a parent's income class, income inequality and risk-based pricing. This is another tool in a war on the poor. Fearing customers will default on their house loan, those with loan-to-value calculations over 80% are routinely required to pay hundreds of dollars more each month to pay for a primary mortgage insurance (PMI) policy that protects the bank in case of default.

Requiring primary mortgage insurance makes a house loan less affordable for lower and middle-income applicants. This higher monthly cost causes some homeowners to default on their mortgage. Again, I speak from personal experience.

As in the loan-to-value argument previously, there are better factors for a financial institution to consider when weighing risk of default. Those factors are DTI, a customer not paying higher risk-based pricing values and a positive credit history of on time payments. If all of those factors are healthy, then the risk of default should be low. Not charging even more money each month for PMI reduces the risk of default even more.

Payday and title loan stores should be required to perform debt-to-income ratio calculations to ensure an applicant can afford the payments on their loan

I understand that many people turn to payday and title loan stores today as a means to receive the credit they would not qualify for at a traditional bank or credit union. Hopefully with the changes we are outlining here, more people will be able to receive bank credit or will not need a loan because they are not being underpaid or overcharged. Regardless, if payday and title loan stores remain in existence it needs to be understood that their customers should only receive credit they can afford to repay.

When payday and title loan stores extend credit that customers cannot afford to repay in the timeframe agreed upon, then the cost for these loans and the chance for financial ruin goes up dramatically. Therefore, payday and title loan stores should have to perform the same debt-to-income calculations as a bank or credit union.

I understand if payday and title loan stores decide not to review credit history. Chances are that the customers that apply with them already have poor credit. If they did not have poor credit they would be better served at other financial institutions and with different products that have more generous loan terms. However, by not determining if a desperate applicant has the ability to repay their loan is like throwing a person off of a boat in the middle of the ocean without asking them if they know how to swim. There is a good chance it will not end well.

Payday and title loan stores should have their maximum interest rates and fees capped

Those customers needing loans from payday and title loan stores are the same people who could not receive the credit they needed from traditional banks and credit unions. Meaning, that a large percentage of this customer base are comprised of people impacted by financial discrimination either through generational poverty or because of income inequality.

Until the financially discriminatory practices of banks and credit unions are corrected there remains a need for payday and title loan stores in poor communities. However, like banks, charging excessive interest rates and fees traps payday and title loan store customers so deeply in debt that many never escape it. That cycle of debt is then passed down to their children like a family heirloom.

The challenge here remains in what is considered excessive as it pertains to interest rates and fees. The standard I would argue is that if you would have paid more in interest and fees than you received in credit (if the cost was annualized), then the price for the loan was excessive.

For example, let's imagine that Christian took out a $400 loan from a payday lending store. He took the loan out for 1 week and ended up paying $20 in fees and interest for the loan. Let's assume he cannot pay the loan back after the first week and it rolls over for another week. This keeps happening and Christian ends up having the loan for a full year (I understand that is not typical policy, but we need to make an apple to apple comparison as it relates to annualized interest rates).

- The fees and interest rate on the $400 loan still cost Christian $20 per week for the entire year.
- Since Christian paid $20 every week for a year in order to have the $400 loan, he paid back a total of $1,040 in fees that could be construed as interest. That equates to a 260% annual percentage rate on the loan.

- Christian had a $400 loan but paid back $1,440 (original loan amount plus interest and fees).

- If you had a one-year car loan for $10,000 and were charged 260% in interest, in 1 year you would end up owing $26,000 in interest, for a full repayment of $36,000 after 1 year. In traditional banking and credit unions we would consider this as excessive and this loan would not be legally allowed.

Because payday and title loan stores extend credit for a short period of time, they typically avoid this same type of annual interest rate comparison to traditional loans. However, their customers are still impacted and get stuck in a cycle of debt because of their high fees. This is why I am urging payday and title loan stores to cap their interest rate and fee charges to an annualized equivalent rate of 100%.

In our example of Christian above, a 100% cap on charges would mean that the most Christian could be charged for a $400 loan would be $7.69 per week.

For those payday and title loan companies that are already keeping their fees and interest rates below the 100% comparative standard, I tip my hat to you. For everyone else, it is time to quit preying on the desperate.

Make a profit, not a killing.

Eliminate bank fees

If bank fees were eliminated entirely it would have an immediate impact on bank profitability. I believe that loss would be partially offset by not having to pay out fines and settlements on related lawsuits. I also believe eliminating risk-based pricing will additionally lead to increased business and therefore the missing bank fee revenue would be replaced by an increase in loan revenue. But there is no denying, looking at only eliminating fees will cost banks a source of revenue. Also, certain fees are used as a deterrent to detrimental financial practices (i.e. overdrawing your checking account).

So, if it might not be in a banks best interest financially to eliminate all bank fees, why am I suggesting it? Bank fees are disproportionately charged to those impacted by discrimination through income inequality. They favor the wealthy with higher balances at the detriment of middle and low-income wage earners. As long as businesses do not pay an equal wage to all employees, bank fee charges are not free of discrimination.

  As for fees being a deterrent for overdrawing an account, that has already been solved for from a technology perspective. Resulting from consumer protections that already went into effect, a bank has to allow a customer to opt out of overdraft fees. Rather than paying a check or allowing money to be withdrawn from an ATM machine if there is not enough money in the account, the bank must have the technology required to reject the transaction. If the transaction is rejected then there is no debit and therefore the account is not overdrawn. This means customers will have to be careful with the checks they write because they may have to pay fees to the businesses that could not cash their checks. But it removes financial institutions from the discriminatory process of charging bank fees disproportionately to low-income customers and those impacted by income inequality.

Banks and credit unions can also return to the old practice of offering a small line of credit to their customers that serves as overdraft protection. These allow overdrafts to be considered and priced as a small loan. This loan rate is still much cheaper for a customer than overdraft fees. Banks moved away from this solution because overdraft fees were more profitable to them.

Mugging me on the sidewalk and stealing my wallet would be more profitable than trying to earn my business. But laws prevent banks from robbing me. That same legal system should protect us from excess and discriminatory bank practices as it relates to fee charges.

Eliminate bank programs that offer special deposit rates and loan rate discounts to their wealthiest customers

Like bank fees, offering special deposit and lending rates based on account balances is a way for banks to use income inequality to financially discriminate against their customers. If not for income inequality this may not be an issue. But when there is unequal pay than benefits tied to income levels is unequal as well.

There are various banking programs that offer these extra rewards. One that has been around for many years and is the easiest to recognize is Private Banking. However, several banks are now moving to these types of programs to win the business of the wealthiest customers. Again, it benefits the rich at the detriment of the poor. It further punishes those facing income inequality by offering better prices to those people that tend to not have to contend with income inequality. In other words, it tends to exclude minorities, women, the differently abled and those making a lower income.

In a perfect world, financial institutions would implement the nine changes detailed in this chapter. They would do it of their own free will because it is the right thing to do and because in many instances, it is the profitable thing to do. History would then remember this period as banking reform.

The first bank that begins to implement these changes will receive all of my business. And I would expect that they would receive the business of many others as well. They would earn a reputation as being on the frontline of banking reform and for being fair and equitable. The additional business should drive up their overall profits.

However, if financial institutions fail to act on these nine changes, then it will be time for customers to make their voices heard and demand change. It will be time for a financial revolt. Ideas on how customers can encourage bank reform will be covered in the next chapter.

Chapter 12

Revolt!

As discussed in the last chapter, my hope is that financial institutions take the initiative to end financial discrimination. My fear is that they will not. In business, profits tend to outweigh ethics and radical changes to tried and true processes requires' real leadership and courage. I have to wonder if there are any courageous leaders left in the banking and financial industry. But where business fails to act in the best interest of others, they can be encouraged to act in their own best interest.

In this chapter I will highlight the steps consumers can take to encourage financial institutions to end financial discrimination. These are easy solutions you and I can implement today. The only challenge is getting enough people to take action; proving to enough people that their lives are made worse by financial discrimination that includes income inequality, classism, racism, sexism or ableism. Every day citizens have the power to fight back, to revolt against the current system.

Below are the highlights of the strategy for financial revolt. Later in the chapter we will describe each of these strategies in more detail:

1. Boycott the institutions that engage in financial discrimination

2. Reward institutions that stop engaging in financial discrimination

3. Write two letters every day; make two phone calls every day

4. Report financial discrimination

5. Sue to protect your rights

6. Targeted strikes and protests

7. Pray

8. Share this book

9. Live

Boycott the institutions that engage in financial discrimination

This can be done today. We do not need an official nationwide boycott to be declared before we each take action. There does not need to be a Twitter hashtag setup or a Facebook page created. However, if someone sees that as a need and feels like taking action, I fully support you.

What we each need to understand is that financial institutions speak the language of money. When their profits are up, they interpret that as the public being supportive of their policies. It is only when their profits are down quarter over quarter or year over year that financial institutions will take notice and consider changing their practices. In other words, we need to speak with our checkbook.

Today, all banks and credit unions are engaging in the type of financial discrimination highlighted throughout this book. I would love to tell you to only do business with those that are not, but then you would not be able to do your banking, cash your paycheck or receive a loan. However, fees are one area where we can already see a difference between banks and credit unions as it relates to factors linked to financial discrimination. Therefore, I believe we lead the boycott based on fees and advance from there.

Here are ways to boycott:

> ➤ Move your checking and/or saving accounts to the bank or credit union in your area that charges the least amount in fees. Not financial

institutions that will waive the fee for maintaining a minimum balance, but rather banks that charge their customers the lowest fees in town for a monthly account service fee, overdrafts, ATM usage, etc.

- When you are at the new bank or credit union opening your account mention that you are looking for a financial institution that:
  ✓ Eliminates Risk-based pricing for loans
  ✓ Stops using credit scores for loan decisions that are not adjusted to account for income inequality
  ✓ Eliminates Primary Mortgage Insurance that is required to be paid by a borrower

- ✓ Eliminates LTV calculations for loans
- ✓ Expands DTI calculations to include discretionary spending
- ✓ Stops charging fees
- ✓ Stops offering special deposit rates and loan pricing for their "most valuable" customers

➢ Try to only submit loan applications to banks or credit unions in your area that charge the least amount in fees.
- When you meet with the banker to submit the loan application, mention that you are looking for a financial institution that will stop the financially discriminatory

practices we just outlined in the last bullet point.

Reward institutions that stop engaging in financial discrimination

Any bank or financial institution that takes action on ending financial discrimination should be rewarded. Therefore, any bank or financial institution that makes changes to policy around the points in this book should receive the deposits and lending business of all citizens concerned with equality. The financial institution that implements all of the changes should keep our business and support. That financial institution should become much more profitable having been rewarded with substantially more deposits and loans.

Write two letters every day; make two phone calls every day

For those that can afford to, each and every day we should send out two hand written letters.

> Letter #1 should be sent to the bank or credit union in your area that charges the highest amount in fees. That letter should state that you prefer they stop:
- ✓ Risk-based pricing for loans
- ✓ Using credit scores for loan decisions that are not adjusted to account for income inequality
- ✓ Primary Mortgage Insurance that is required to be paid by the borrower
- ✓ LTV calculations for loans
- ✓ Limiting DTI calculations
- ✓ Charging fees
- ✓ Offering special deposit rates and loan pricing for their most valuable customers

➢ Letter #2 should be sent to the senator that represents you in government. Go to the **Congress.gov** website to research which member of congress represents your area and their mailing address. In that letter state that you prefer they pass laws to end financial discrimination at our banks and financial institutions. Those financially discriminatory policies are:
- ✓ Risk-based pricing for loans
- ✓ Using credit scores for loan decisions that are not adjusted to account for income inequality
- ✓ Primary Mortgage Insurance that is required to be paid by the borrower
- ✓ LTV calculations for loans
- ✓ Limiting DTI calculations
- ✓ Charging fees

- ✓ Offering special deposit rates and loan pricing for their most valuable customers

Call #1 should be to the bank you mailed your letter to. Call each and every day to ensure they received your letter from the day before.

Call #2 should be to the senator you mailed your letter to. Call each day to ensure they received your letter the day before.

Daily letters and calls are hard to ignore. They are a legal and peaceful way to have your voice heard and to limit the amount of financially discriminatory work that can be done for the day by a bank or financial institution or a dismissive senator.

Report financial discrimination

If you are denied a loan or offered different lending terms because of a financially discriminatory reason, submit a complaint with the Consumer Financial Protection Bureau. Current definitions of what constitutes financial discrimination may limit action. But with every voice heard we get closer to redefining financial discrimination and having it reflect truth. So, submit a complaint if:

> ➢ You are impacted by income inequality and you are denied a loan or forced to pay a subprime rate because your debt-to-income ratio calculation was too high.

> ➢ You are impacted by income inequality and you are denied a loan or forced to pay a subprime rate because your loan-to-value ratio calculation was too high.

- You are impacted by income inequality and you are denied a loan or forced to pay a subprime rate because of your credit score. Remember that these scores should be adjusted to reflect the discrimination you already receive through income inequality.

- You are impacted by income inequality and you are forced to pay for primary mortgage insurance.

- You are impacted by income inequality and are taking out a payday or title loan and are being charged more than 100% interest on an annualized adjusted rate when including both fees and interest rates.

Sue to protect your rights

In the cases defined above, when your rights have been violated by policies reflecting financial discrimination, you can choose to hire an attorney and sue for damages. Again, impacting a financial institutions profit is the best way to get their attention. Sometimes all it takes is the threat of a lawsuit to change policy.

Targeted strikes and protests

For anyone impacted by income inequality, strikes and protests are ways of getting your voice heard. My fear here is that those making less money because of income inequality are also those that can least afford taking time off to protest. A business with millions or billions of dollars can turn a deaf ear to a protestor who has only enough money saved to strike for a short time. That is why I believe in targeted strikes.

A targeted strike is the right person or industry striking to maximize impact. In this case I would call on bankers to stand up for those impacted by financial discrimination in their banks and credit unions. Many of these bankers are doing like the rest of us, executing company policy because they need a job. Many of them are also impacted by income inequality and feel strongly about equal pay and equal treatment and equal opportunities. Now is the time to prove it.

All bankers responsible for submitting loans are on the front line in the battle against financial discrimination. If they wish to fight for the ending of classist, racist, sexist and ableist behavior by their banks and credit unions then they can do so through the lending process. They should counsel their customers to not sign the lending contract if the customer does not receive the best interest rate available because they are impacted by income inequality based on their economic class, race, sex or because they are differently abled.

If a customer is denied a loan because of income inequality impacting credit scores, debt-to-income or loan-to-value calculations, then the banker should recommend that the customer submit a complaint with the Consumer Financial Protection Bureau, as described in the section above concerning reporting financial discrimination.

If any bankers are reprimanded or terminated because they are taking this stand against financial discrimination, then I believe a protest outside of that bank is appropriate. I would ask that any and all peoples, who have the financial means and that are concerned with equality, join in the protest to defend the moral banker and to make a stand against financial discrimination within our banks and credit unions.

Pray

God still moves mountains. With God all things are still possible.

Share this book

There is a lot of technical detail in this book and that can be hard to relay to others when you do not have a banking or financial background. I recommend sharing the book with your local banker, send a copy to your state representative, send a copy to your friends and family…anything to lend your voice to ending financial discrimination.

Live

From personal experience I know that money trouble leads to stress, depressed thoughts, pain and even thoughts of suicide. When you cannot pay your bills or feel that you cannot provide enough for your family, those negative thoughts and feelings can turn into regrettable actions. You begin to think that no one understands how you feel and that no one cares to help. But you are wrong.

As I stated before, an estimated 41 million people lived in poverty in 2016 in the United States

(United States Census Bureau, 2017). You are not alone.

- As long as businesses pay an unequal income…you will not be alone in your financial suffering.

- As long as financial institutions do not eliminate the impact of financial discrimination in their policy decisions… you will not be alone in your financial suffering.

- As long as congress does not pass effective laws to prevent financial discrimination… you will not be alone in your financial suffering.

You are not alone and together we can take action to force effective change.

Despite our feelings of isolation, we need to pull together. We need to stand up for one another and demand financial equality for all people. You were "fearfully and wonderfully made". You are priceless even if some do not understand your full value.

Where there is life there is hope. So, I would ask that you live and stand with me in demanding changes to our financial institutions that will minimize or eliminate financial discrimination. Barring bank reform, it is time to revolt!

Chapter 13

Just the Beginning

Throughout the chapters in this book we have identified discriminatory practices being executed daily in all banks and financial institutions in the United States of America. We have also reviewed solutions that banks and financial institutions can take to eliminate these unfair practices while working towards increasing their profits. The previous chapter focused on what customers can do to encourage banks to reform their discriminatory practices.

I believe that financial institutions have a constitutional responsibility to:

1. Provide equal access to all financial services without exclusion based on a person's economic class, race, sex or if they are differently abled.

2. Provide equal terms for all loans and deposit products without variance based on a person's economic class, race, sex or if they are differently abled.

   ➢ Because of income inequality and current policies, I believe that financial institutions are failing to meet both of these constitutional responsibilities.

Resolving income inequality will take more than just the efforts of financial institutions. It will require courageous leadership and change from all of our institutions:

   ➢ Government officials
   ➢ School boards
   ➢ Religious leaders
   ➢ Business leaders

Ending income inequality will also require hard work and sacrifice by ordinary citizens.

- Make your voice heard
- Only spend your hard-earned money with businesses that reflect your values
- Fight for a quality education for everyone
- If you already manage a business or can start one of your own – hire, pay and promote fairly

As gatekeepers to our financial system, banks and financial institutions can negate much of the negative consequences of income inequality. They can also take steps to eliminate additional policies that also discriminate against citizens based on economic class, race, sex and physical ability:

➤ Eliminate risk-based pricing

- Adjust minimum credit scores for loan approvals to reflect income inequality

- Expand debt-to-income calculations

- Eliminate loan-to-value ratio calculations as a deciding factor for loan approvals

- Eliminate borrower paid Primary Mortgage Insurance

- Eliminate bank fees

- Eliminate special deposit and lending pricing programs that are discriminatory

- Cap interest rates and fees for payday and title loan stores

To see real change in our financial system we need brave people who believe in justice, to be supported by those that are courageous.

Those brave people that stand against financial discrimination because they are impacted by its damaging effects, they seek justice. They must demand a fair system for themselves as well as for their children and grandchildren. The status quo will not work for them because it has never worked for them. They cannot accept just surviving when they were created to be "more than conquerors".

Those that stand against financial discrimination even though they are not greatly impacted by it, or maybe they even benefit from it, they must be courageous. They must be willing to stand up for the rights God gave us all. They must stand up for the rights granted and guaranteed to all U.S. citizens under the Constitution.

Remember that we grow best when we grow together.

Financial discrimination limits the potential of our citizens, impacts the profitability of financial institutions and businesses and restrains our economy. If we truly want to be the world leader in prosperity and innovation, then we have to quit restraining the potential of our population through financial discrimination.

Change is never easy. It takes courage. It requires sacrifice. There is a cost to break away from the familiar and to embrace new and innovative processes. But there is also a cost for inaction. We are paying those costs now by not living up to our full potential as a people and as an economy.

I am sure that many of the people in our country that benefit from the current system of income inequality and financial discrimination will insult the points raised in this book. They will stand up for the current system. They will deny that there is an issue. They will use their influence to try and convince those that are being discriminated against that there is truly no problem. They will say that the Titanic is not sinking, while they themselves enjoy spacious seating in the lifeboat of their own wealth. I expect criticism. I expect ridicule. However, I cannot sit silently and say nothing or else I too am at fault for supporting a corrupt system.

I have worked in banking and finance. I have calculated the debt-to-incomes and loan-to-values. I have had to deny loans. I have had to deny fee refunds. I have a personal connection to the struggles of the differently abled. I have been a customer who paid subprime loan rates. I have skipped meals to pay higher loan payments. I paid for Primary Mortgage Insurance for a decade. I have lost my electricity, my water, my heat. I have sat on the floor of my repossessed house and contemplated suicide, wondering if I could ever look my wife and children in the eyes again. There is an issue. The Titanic has sprung a leak. The privileged are pacifying you even while they steal your wallet. Financial discrimination against anyone is a crime against everyone.

Some of you may say that we do not have to take action because of survival of the fittest and that those that deserve to thrive, will. Millions of Americans are being financially discriminated against daily. They are black, Hispanic, Asian, white, male, female, veterans of the armed forces, the differently abled. When they find their voices, when they stop crying and start to grow angry, when they finalize realize they are being pitted against each other by left and right leaning interest groups, when they finally realize they have the power, then you will see who is the most "fit". We are a nation planted through rebellion and watered by blood. A nation founded by ticked off people who wanted to escape from oppression. So, when we oppress, we forfeit our birthright. Historically, when we have repressed the rights of individuals, there has been war.

I know the message of this book will be hard to accept. My greatest fear is not that it will be ridiculed but rather ignored. However, discrimination in our financial institutions is impossible to ignore. It is experienced daily in every bank and credit union. It has become legal, accepted and profitable. But it is still wrong. It is better for our citizens, our businesses and our country if we right this wrong now.

I pray financial institutions will reform. If not by implementing the changes detailed in this book, then by making other changes that negate discrimination in the financial industry. If they do not, I pray people will speak up in overwhelming numbers and demand change.

Now is the time for either Reform or Revolt!

About the Author

I am an American author who lives in the Midwest with my wife and three children. I gained the knowledge to write this book in completing my MBA with a perfect 4.0 GPA. I have gained the expertise to write this book after spending over 16 years working in the financial industry. During that time, I worked in various roles in banking, taught Business Finance and Accounting classes and ran my own business as a Financial Adviser. Most recently I was a Vice President of one of the largest banks in the world.

In my banking career, I have worked my way up from a teller role to opening new accounts, submitting and deciding loan applications, managing investment accounts and eventually to a manager of multiple branch locations. In my final role in banking, I was a Sr. Business Control Specialist responsible for process design and issue identification and remediation over banking services.

In this last role as Vice President, it was my responsibility to identify when banking processes were not working as ideally as they could. I would then design solutions and implement changes as needed. This book is a continuation of that effort to improve banking processes and make them more profitable for financial institutions as well as more equitable for all of their customers.

Email me at bendavis9@hotmail.com. Follow me on Twitter @inaislin.

Bibliography

American Institutes for Research. (2014, Dec 14). Those with disabilities earn 37% less on average; gap is even wider in some states. *American Institutes for Research*. Retrieved from https://www.air.org/news/press-release/those-disabilities-earn-37-less-average-gap-even-wider-some-states

Bocian, D. G., Ernst, K., & Li, W. (2010, Jun). Foreclosures by race and ethnicity: the demographics of a crisis. *Center for Responsible Lending*. Retrieved from https://www.responsiblelending.org/mortgage-lending/research-analysis/foreclosures-by-race-and-ethnicity.pdf

Bourke, N. (2016, Jan 14). Payday loan facts and the CFPB's impact. *The PEW Charitable Trusts*. Retrieved from https://www.pewtrusts.org/en/research-and-analysis/fact-sheets/2016/01/payday-loan-facts-and-the-cfpbs-impact

FDIC. (2018, Feb 27). Press release: FDIC-insured institutions report net income of $25.5 billion in fourth quarter 2017. *FDIC.* Retrieved from https://www.fdic.gov/news/news/press/2018/pr18013.pdf

FDIC. (2015, Sep). Fair lending laws and regulations. *FDIC.* Retrieved from https://www.fdic.gov/regulations/compliance/manual/4/iv-1.1.pdf

Kraus, L., Lauer, E., Coleman, R., and Houtenville, A. (2018). 2017 disability statistics annual report. *Disability Compendium.* Retrieved from https://disabilitycompendium.org/sites/default/files/user-uploads/2017_AnnualReport_FINAL.pdf

RealtyTrac. (2018, Jun). U.S. real estate trends & market info. *RealtyTrac.* Retrieved from https://www.realtytrac.com/statsandtrends/foreclosuretrends/

Senega, J., Fontenot, K.R., & Kollar, M. (2017, Sep). Income and poverty in the United States:2016. *United States Census Bureau.* Retrieved from https://www.census.gov/content/dam/Census/library/publications/2017/demo/P60-259.pdf

United States Census Bureau. (2017, Jul 1). Quick facts United states. *U.S. Department of Commerce.* Retrieved from https://www.census.gov/quickfacts/fact/table/US/IPE120218#viewtop

United States Census Bureau. (2018, Apr 26). Homeownership rates by race and ethnicity of householder: 2014 to 2018. *U.S. Department of Commerce.* Retrieved from https://www.census.gov/housing/hvs/files/currenthvspress.pdf

www.ingramcontent.com/pod-product-compliance
Lightning Source LLC
Chambersburg PA
CBHW031618210526
45464CB00004B/1642